HOW TO HELP

Beginning Teachers Succeed

2ND EDITION

STEPHEN P. GORDON
and
SUSAN MAXEY

Association for Supervision and Curriculum Development
Alexandria, Virginia USA

Association for Supervision and Curriculum Development
1703 N. Beauregard St. • Alexandria, VA 22311-1714 USA
Telephone: 1-800-933-2723 or 703-578-9600 • Fax: 703-575-5400
Web site: http://www.ascd.org • E-mail: member@ascd.org

Gene R. Carter, *Executive Director and Chief Executive Officer*
Michelle Terry, *Deputy Executive Director, Program Development*
Nancy Modrak, *Director, Publishing*
John O'Neil, *Director of Acquisitions*
Julie Houtz, *Managing Editor of Books*
Darcie Russell, *Associate Editor*
Gary Bloom, *Director, Design and Production Services*
Karen Monaco, *Senior Designer*
W. Keith Demmons, *Graphic Designer*
Tracey A. Smith, *Production Manager*
Dina Murray Seamon, *Production Coordinator*

ASCD publications present a variety of viewpoints. The views expressed or implied in this
book should not be interpreted as official positions of the Association.

Printed in the United States of America.

ASCD Product No. 100217
ASCD member price: $10.95   nonmember price: $13.95
s9/00

Library of Congress Cataloging-in-Publication Data

Gordon, Stephen P., 1948-
  How to help beginning teachers succeed / Stephen P. Gordon and Susan
Maxey.— 2nd ed.
      p. cm.
Includes bibliographical references and index.
"ASCD stock no. 0010021700"—T.p. verso.
  ISBN 0-87120-382-0
  1. First year teachers—United States—Handbooks, manuals, etc. I.
Maxey, Susan, 1963- II. Title.
  LB2844.1.N4 G67 2000
  371.1—dc21   00-009613

06 05 04 03 02 01   10 9 8 7 6 5 4 3 2

How to Help Beginning Teachers Succeed

2nd Edition

1 The Problem: Unforeseen Difficulties

I sat by the same person every single day at lunch, and I never really talked to him. He wouldn't even say hello to me. Sometimes I would walk into the faculty lounge, and it was just like there was a wall between me and the older teachers.

—A BEGINNING TEACHER

In the coming year, thousands of college graduates will enter the nation's classrooms to begin their teaching careers. Most of these teachers will have received high grades in their teaching methods courses and student teaching experiences. Most will have a genuine affection for young people and will be committed to making a difference in the lives of their students. Despite the good intentions and high expectations of these beginners, 40 to 50 percent of them will drop out of teaching within the first seven years (New Mexico State Department of Education, 1988; Wisconsin Department of Public Instruction, 1984; Thomas & Kiley, 1994), most within the first two years (Schlechty & Vance, 1983). Of those who survive, many will have such negative initial experiences that they may never reach their full potential as educators (Romatowski, Dorminey, & Voorhees, 1989; Huling-Austin, 1986).

Six Environmental Difficulties

What is the cause of the alarming attrition rate in the early years of teaching? Some blame the quality of those who enter teaching, others point to the teacher education programs that prepare them. The literature, however, indicates that many of the difficulties beginners encounter are environmental in nature; they are grounded in the culture of the teaching profession and the conditions of the school as a workplace. Let's look at six environmental difficulties that await our novice teachers.

1. Difficult Work Assignments

Other professions gradually increase the novice's work responsibilities over time. In the teaching profession, beginners often start out with more responsibilities than veteran teachers and are expected to perform all of their duties with the same expertise as experienced professionals. Returning teachers usually choose to teach the best courses, leaving the least interesting and most difficult courses to beginners (Kurtz, 1983). New teachers are often given the most time-consuming and least rewarding assignments (Kurtz, 1983) as well as larger classes, more difficult students, and more duties than experienced teachers (Romatowski, Dorminey, & Voorhees, 1989). New teachers are often given assignments like lunch duty, bus duty, monitoring after school detentions, and coordinating the less popular extracurricular activities.

2. Unclear Expectations

Schools have myriad formal rules and procedures that are new and unclear to beginning teachers. Beyond formal expectations, there are many informal routines and customs that are even more difficult for new teachers to learn. To make matters more complicated, different groups expect different things from beginners (Niebrand, Horn, & Holmes, 1992; Corley, 1998). Conflicting expectations of administrators, other teachers, students, and parents contribute to what Corcoran has referred to as the "condition of not knowing" (1981, p. 20). A study of first-year teachers (Kurtz, 1983) revealed that a common complaint of novice teachers was "I never knew what was expected of me." This complaint was most common among those who left teaching early.

3. Inadequate Resources

Entry-year teachers often find their classrooms lacking instructional resources and materials (Gratch, 1998). In many cases this is because of the traditional "summer raid" on classrooms belonging to recently resigned teachers:

> When a teacher resigns, the remaining teachers often descend upon the classroom and remove any materials, equipment, or furniture of value and replace them with their discards. The new teacher enters a classroom equipped with leftovers (Glickman, 1984-85, p. 38).

The effects of such raiding on beginning teachers can be frustrating and harmful. When teachers are most in need of quality instructional resources and materials they often have the worst in the school.

4. Isolation

Beginning teachers often suffer from emotional isolation when they are assigned to the most physically isolated classrooms (Kurtz, 1983). They may also suffer from social and professional isolation (Dussault et al., 1997). Experienced teachers are not likely to offer assistance to beginning teachers, even when beginners are clearly experiencing severe difficulties (Houston & Felder, 1982; Ryan,

1979; Newberry, 1978). Why do experienced teachers avoid assisting new teachers? Some believe that beginning teachers need to go through their rites of passage alone, just as the veterans did in their first years (Ryan, 1979). Others would like to offer assistance to new teachers but feel their efforts would be viewed as interference. Many experienced teachers feel that the principal alone is responsible for assisting new teachers.

Beginning teachers contribute to their own isolation when they hesitate to ask for help. Many consider seeking help an admission of failure and incompetence. In fact, beginning teachers studied by Newberry (1978) went to great lengths to cover up serious problems with student discipline.

5. Role Conflict

It is true that growing numbers of adults in their late twenties, thirties, and beyond are now entering or reentering teaching, but the majority of beginning teachers continue to be young adults. Conflict often exists between the roles of teacher and young adult. The new teacher may be living away from home or the safety of college for the first time and may have just moved to a new community. He may be opening bank or charge accounts, renting and furnishing an apartment, or buying a car for the first time. He may be beginning a marriage or starting a family. A nonteaching spouse may be unable to relate to the teacher's concerns about what is happening at school or understand why he spends so much more time and energy on schoolwork than on the family. The conflict between the roles of teacher and young adult often leads new teachers to perceive that neither role is being given sufficient time and attention. This perception can lead to strong feelings of guilt (Gehrke, 1982) and unhappiness.

6. Reality Shock

According to Veenman, "reality shock" is "the collapse of the missionary ideals formed during teacher training by the harsh and rude reality of classroom life" (1984, p. 143). It is caused by the beginning teacher's realizations about the world of teaching and her lack of preparation for many of the demands and difficulties of that world. Many beginners embark on their first teaching assignments with highly idealized perceptions of teaching: They tend to envision themselves spending the entire day fostering their students' academic growth. Early on, they find that teaching actually includes a wide range of nonacademic duties, including disciplining students, collecting money and forms, completing administrative paperwork, and serving as substitute parents. Additionally, teachers who have looked forward to being autonomous, creative professionals may find their orientation toward teaching in conflict with prescribed curricula, instructional programs, textbooks, or materials (Braga, 1972). The discrepancy between the beginning teacher's vision of teaching and the real world of teaching can cause serious disillusionment (Armstrong, 1984; Braga, 1972; Campbell, 1972; Osbourne, 1992; Cameron, 1994; Jesus & Paixao, 1996). Corcoran (1981) found that "transition shock" can lead to a state of paralysis that renders teachers unable to transfer to the classroom the skills they learned during teacher education. Reality shock can make the other five environmental difficulties more severe by reducing a beginning teacher's ability to cope.

Twelve Potential Needs

The specific problems and needs of beginning teachers have been the focus of several studies (Boccia, 1991, 1989; Odell, Loughlin, & Ferraro, 1986-1987; Veenman, 1984; Grant & Zeichner, 1981;

Johnston & Ryan, 1980; Corley, 1998). Although no two studies have produced precisely the same lists of problems or needs, the studies that yield prioritized lists of problems or needs tend to have the same items at the top of each list (although the specific order varies). Thus, a set of potential high-priority needs of beginning teachers is suggested by the research. Many beginning teachers need help with

- Managing the classroom.
- Acquiring information about the school system.
- Obtaining instructional resources and materials.
- Planning, organizing, and managing instruction, as well as other professional responsibilities.
- Assessing students and evaluating student progress.
- Motivating students.
- Using effective teaching methods.
- Dealing with individual students' needs, interests, abilities, and problems.
- Communicating with colleagues, including administrators, supervisors, and other teachers.
- Communicating with parents.
- Adjusting to the teaching environment and role.
- Receiving emotional support.

Many of these specific needs are rooted in one or more of the environmental difficulties discussed earlier. At the same time, insufficient knowledge, skill, experience, and socialization can contribute to these needs. Therefore, *both* the environmental difficulties and specific needs of beginners must be addressed. These needs should not be adopted automatically as the needs list for your district's assistance program. Your teachers may have vital needs that differ from those of the general population of beginning teachers. In reality, each new teacher probably has some needs similar to most begin-

ning teachers everywhere, some needs unique to the group of beginners in the same specific work setting, and some needs unique to
that teacher alone. Your beginning teacher assistance program
development committee should conduct a local needs assessment
before defining and prioritizing beginners' needs. Also, the induction team (see Chapter 2) for each beginner should be given the
flexibility to identify and meet individual needs.

Effects of Unmet Needs

If the environmental difficulties and specific needs of beginning
teachers are not addressed, negative emotional, physical, attitudinal,
and behavioral problems may result (Cameron, 1994; Dussault et al.,
1997; Schmidt & Knowles, 1994). The beginner may suffer from
insomnia or nightmares (Applegate et al., 1977), leading to fatigue
and physical exhaustion or a sense of failure and depression (Ryan et
al., 1980). Outbursts of crying, loss of temper, and occasional
vomiting are not uncommon (Ryan, 1974).

Novice teachers' early experiences are likely to lower their self-
esteem, make them less optimistic, and cause them to develop negative attitudes toward children (Earp & Tanner, 1975). They tend to
view themselves as less happy, less relaxed, less confident, less
perceptive, more controlled, and more blaming than they were
before they started teaching (Wright & Tuska, 1968). They often
feel they possess less knowledge about teaching at the end than at
the beginning of their first year (Gaede, 1978) and see themselves as
becoming more authoritarian, dominating, and custodial in their
treatment of students (Day, 1959; Hoy, 1969, 1968; McArthur,
1978). Beginners report that they become more impulsive, less
inspiring, louder, less responsive, more reserved, and make school
more boring as a result of their early teaching experiences (Wright
& Tuska, 1968). Some of these changes are the result of beginners'

frustration with their teaching not seeming to result in student learning. Other changes are responses to problems with classroom management.

What is the ultimate effect of negative experiences reported by beginning teachers? They exit the profession. The attrition rate for each of the first two years of teaching is about 15 percent, compared to a normal turnover rate of 6 percent within the teaching profession (Schlechty & Vance, 1983). Moreover, studies show that it is the most promising teachers who leave teaching in the early years (Harris & Collay, 1990; Schlechty & Vance, 1983) and many teachers who survive the induction period and remain in teaching develop a survival mentality, a set of restricted teaching methods, and a resistance to curricular and instructional change that may last throughout their teaching careers (Romatowski, Dorminey, & Voorhees, 1989; Huling-Austin, 1986).

* * *

Many of the problems associated with beginning teachers may not be present in your school system. Staff members charged with developing programs to assist beginning teachers have a responsibility to take a hard look at the beginning teacher literature and compare it to the environment and experiences of beginning teachers in their schools.

2 The Solution: A Beginning Teacher Assistance Program

She's very understanding and compassionate. I know that whenever I have a problem, I can call her at home or I can see her after school and she'll always take the time to talk to me. She always gives me that positive reinforcement, that pat on the back.

—A BEGINNING TEACHER DISCUSSING HER MENTOR

A discussion of what a beginning teacher assistance program (BTAP) is usually leads to a discussion about the definition of "beginning teacher." Is the experienced substitute teacher who has just been hired for her first regular teaching assignment a beginner? What about the person who is returning after several years? How about the experienced teacher who is new to the district, building, content area, or grade level? Most likely, all of these teachers need some special assistance, but the support they require is different from the support needed by the true novice. Questions like "What should be the goals of the assistance program?", "Who will be served by the program?", "How long will individuals be part of the program?", and "What types of support are most appropriate for different types of 'beginners'?" are best dealt with at the local level. When answering these questions, the local development team must consider variables such as the goals of the school district's staff development program, the district's resources, and the types and numbers of beginning teachers in the district.

What a BTAP Is and Is Not

A BTAP can be defined as a formal, systematic effort to provide ongoing assistance to a new teacher during the induction period. Many educators believe that it takes up to three years to fully induct a beginning teacher and that some type of formal assistance should be provided to the beginner throughout that time.

Huling-Austin (1988) identified five commonly accepted goals of teacher induction programs:

1. To improve teaching performance.
2. To increase the retention of promising beginning teachers.
3. To promote the personal and professional well-being of beginning teachers.
4. To transmit the culture of the system to beginning teachers.
5. To satisfy mandated requirements related to induction and certification.

These five goals are laudable. If the last goal, however, is the only one adopted by a school district, then there is a good chance that a perfunctory program will result, aimed at satisfying the letter rather than the spirit of the mandate. The first four purposes are interrelated and interdependent. They could and should all be integrated into a BTAP that would also satisfy a state mandate for an induction program.

While considering the components of a BTAP, it's also important to understand what a BTAP is not.

- *It is not a beginners' orientation alone.* Some individuals consider an orientation the primary component of a BTAP.

Although an orientation to the school and community is vital, it should be viewed as the entry point, not end point, of teacher induction. It is the long-range, ongoing assistance that is the most important aspect of an effective program.

• *It is not merely the assignment of a buddy.* In many schools, beginning teachers are assigned a buddy who shows the new teacher where to procure supplies and materials and how to fill out various administrative forms. The buddy is also generally available should the beginner seek advice. Usually these buddies have no preparation in the skills needed to assist a beginner. After the first few weeks, interaction between buddy and newcomer tends to be infrequent. The buddy may never even visit the beginner's classroom to observe a lesson. Although such buddy systems are better than no support at all, they should not be confused with a comprehensive BTAP involving an induction team or even with the ongoing assistance provided by a well-prepared mentor. In a study by Klug and Salzman (1991), participants preferred a highly structured program with an induction team including a mentor, administrator, and representative from higher education over a loosely structured buddy system.

• *It is not an evaluation program.* The purpose of a BTAP is purely supportive. It should never be used to identify incompetent teachers. Certainly new teachers must be evaluated and incompetent teachers without potential for improvement should not be allowed to remain in the profession. However, the trust-building, nurturing, and support that are at the core of BTAPs do not mix with the gatekeeping function.

• *It is not a cure-all.* Huling-Austin (1986) reminds us that a BTAP cannot be expected to overcome major problems within the school such as misplaced teachers, overloaded teaching schedules, and overcrowded classes. Nor can the assistance program be expected to turn teachers without potential into competent professionals. It is important that those involved with BTAPs understand the limitations and the potential of the programs.

The Induction Team

The most important ingredients in any beginning teacher assistance program are the people who give their time and energy as part of the induction effort. An induction team is more likely to provide for a beginner's success than a support person operating alone. Several agencies and individuals can be significant players on the induction team.

School Board Members and the Superintendent. These individuals are central to the school district's commitment to the BTAP. They provide the political base and moral support for the program. The superintendent can assist the BTAP development team in finding necessary human and material resources. The school board members and superintendent are also in the best positions to publicly acknowledge those who devote time and energy to assisting beginning teachers.

The Local Education Association. The support of the local education association is important. Because both the school district and the association benefit from a successful BTAP, gaining the support of the association is not usually a problem if the association is involved from the very beginning and if the school district is willing to provide appropriate resources for the BTAP.

The education association can appoint a representative to the BTAP development team and assist in providing preparation and support for mentors. It can also help plan and deliver information and support activities for beginning teachers. Association representatives should be part of the monitoring, evaluation, and revision of the BTAP.

The Principal. The principal's leadership is essential to the BTAP. A common practice is for principals to have the right of approval over mentor appointments and assignments. By attending mentor preparation sessions, principals provide support for the mentors and refine their own knowledge and skills. By attending orientations, workshops, and seminars for beginning teachers, building administrators communicate the high priority they assign to beginning teachers and the assistance program. Building principals should not let the fact that mentors have been assigned to beginning teachers deter them from regularly observing and conferring with new teachers.

The Mentor. In many assistance programs, the beginner is assigned a mentor. The mentor has primary responsibility for providing direct assistance to the new teacher. Sheehy (1976, p. 31) defines a mentor as a "nonparental career model who actively provides assistance, support, and opportunities for the protégé." Alleman, Cochran, Doverspike, and Newman (1984, p. 329) define mentoring as "a relationship in which a person of greater rank or expertise teaches, guides, and develops a novice in an organization or profession." Schmidt and Wolfe (1980) list three broad functions of mentors: role model, consultant-advisor, and sponsor. Schein (1978) has proposed eight possible mentor functions: confidant, teacher, sponsor, role model, developer of talent, opener of doors, protector, and successful leader.

In BTAPs, the mentor is usually an experienced practicing teacher, but others can serve as effective mentors. For example, retired teachers serve as mentors in some assistance programs. The role of the mentor is to support and challenge, but not to evaluate, the beginning teacher. This means that the mentor should not be in a linear relationship with the beginner on the school district's organizational chart.

Central Office Supervisors. A central office supervisor is a likely candidate for coordinator of the district's beginning teacher assistance program. Curriculum development and subject matter coordinators can provide information on the scope and sequence of the curriculum and available curricular resources. Coordinators of special education programs can help beginners to better serve children with special needs. Finally, instructional supervisors can coach mentors in interpersonal, observation, conferencing, and problem-solving skills.

Other Teachers. The department chair or instructional team leader can work with mentors to provide assistance to beginning teachers. These instructional leaders may have areas of expertise different from and complementary to the mentor's. Teacher-leaders can encourage other teachers in the department or on the instructional team to form a support network for the new teacher.

Regular teachers can go a long way toward reducing the beginning teacher's isolation by making a point of regularly interacting with the newcomer. Effective, experienced teachers can allow beginners to visit their classrooms and observe them teaching. All of the teachers in proximity to the beginner can make a commitment to the caring, supportive environment that can give him the optimal chance for success. The idea is that one teacher is the assigned mentor, but all teachers are support teachers.

Teacher Educators. Teacher educators from colleges and universities may be called on for assistance during the planning, implementation, or evaluation phase of the BTAP. The most effective assistance is probably provided by university or college consultants who work with the school district through all of these phases. Specific functions of teacher educators are consulting with the assistance program development team, training and consulting mentors, facilitating group seminars for mentors or beginning teachers, and conducting research on teacher induction.

State Agencies. State agencies can offer guidelines, resources, and consultation to school districts developing BTAPs. They can provide preparation programs for program coordinators and mentor trainers and disseminate information about model programs. State agencies can help school systems organize into consortiums. These consortiums enable school systems to combine resources and offer services to mentors or beginning teachers that they would be unable to provide independently.

School-University Partnerships

Schools and universities entering partnerships to create beginning teacher assistance programs is an exciting trend. A relationship between many schools and universities is already in place because of student teaching (Liebert, 1989). University involvement in teacher induction is logical because university personnel are familiar with the needs of beginning teachers. Also, because the university is not responsible for the evaluation of inductees, they can focus on assisting and supporting all members of the school-based team (Liebert, 1989). The partnership is advantageous for the university because it helps to keep the university's education staff familiar with the functioning of schools and keeps them connected with the problems that real teachers face. Additionally, the university can acquire feedback on how well their programs are preparing students for teaching.

Universities can provide differing levels of support to a school. Some offer minimal support by simply making a university staff member a part of the induction team. Others are intensively involved in activities such as teachers' fellows programs. A description of two different, yet effective, programs follows.

The Kansas Goals 2000 Early Career Professional Development Program provides assistance to teachers in their first three years of experience. This program is a partnership among Pittsburg State University, Emporia State University, the Southeast Education Service Center, and 68 school districts. This well-defined and organized program relies heavily on trained mentors who provide daily support to new teachers (Runyon, White, Hazel, & Hedges, 1998). The mentor's role is clearly defined: the mentor is expected to be an experienced teacher who understands the needs and concerns of beginning teachers and who uses such methods as peer coaching techniques and conferencing skills to help novices. Mentors receive intensive training through sessions and manuals created by the university. The university gives intensive and ongoing support to the mentors. The beginning teachers also receive ongoing training and manuals. Throughout the school year, new teachers participate in seminars and discussions related to various aspects of their first-year concerns (Runyon, White, Hazel, & Hedges, 1998).

The program was planned by university personnel and is implemented at the service center level. It is funded by the universities, through grant money, and by a fee charged to participating school districts. The evaluation of the program has been positive. Both mentors and new teachers have praised the support that they receive throughout the program (Runyon, White, Hazel, & Hedges, 1998).

In California, the Collaborative Learning Network is a program that supports teachers from preservice through their first three years of teaching. This program is a collaboration among California State University, Ontario-Montclair School District and its consortium districts. Working together, university personnel, principals, and teachers determined the weaknesses in teacher education programs. The result is a three-tiered program (Robbins & Skillings, 1996).

The first phase of the program is called Undergraduate Service Learning. In this phase, potential teacher candidates are recruited while in college, and they receive college credit for working in elementary and middle school classrooms. The emphasis is on recruiting students from programs such as math and science, not education (Robbins & Skillings, 1996).

Phase two is called Project Genesis. For an entire school year, student teachers are placed at a site where they follow the school calendar and work with teachers. At the same time, the student teachers take courses taught at the school site by university personnel. The combination of learning and practical experience while working with a mentor teacher is valuable scaffolding. The student teachers benefit from classroom experience as they take courses on teaching methodology and classroom management. Another dimension of this phase is that the experienced teachers receive mentor training through campus-based university classes (Robbins & Skillings, 1996).

In phase three, Project Learn, first-year teachers are assigned mentors. The mentors and new teachers are expected to work together for two years. During this time, the new teachers gain opportunities to observe master teachers and to be observed by them. In addition, the first-year teachers attend pertinent workshops and develop individual growth goals. The program provides 20 hours of release time for mentors to work with new teachers (Robbins & Skillings, 1996).

Kansas Goals 2000 and the Collaborative Learning Network are only two of the many school-university partnerships for beginning teacher assistance programs in the country. These programs can be powerful in helping train and retain new teachers.

Team Members' Involvement

We have taken a look at several potential members of a BTAP development team. All potential members, individuals and agencies, have the potential to assist as well as benefit from a BTAP. The BTAP development team should decide which stakeholders will be part of the assistance program, as well as the extent to which each participant will be involved.

Clear communication among the principal, mentor, and other support persons and agencies is essential. Before the school year begins, the principal and mentors need to meet with other instructional leaders and teachers who will be working with the newcomers to set up procedures for coordinating support efforts. Continued coordination throughout the school year is vital to the success of the program.

Effects of BTAPs in General

An effective BTAP can eliminate many of the problems encountered by beginning teachers. In a cooperative venture between Indiana State University and 10 school districts in West Central Indiana, 20 first-year teachers were assigned an experienced support teacher, received monthly visits from a university supervisor, attended monthly peer-support seminars, and received a newsletter. The interns involved in the program displayed significantly better performance than a control group in 40 teaching skills. The beginners "completed the year with significantly healthier attitudes and perceptions about teaching than did a similar group of beginning teachers who did not have the . . . support program" (Henry, 1988, p. 15). All of the new teachers enrolled in the program chose to stay in teaching.

Parker (1988) studied the Wisconsin-Whitewater Teacher Induction Program, a regional teacher induction program for rural schools. Beginning teacher assistance included peer support from other new teachers, seminars, and an induction team including mentors, school administrators, and university personnel. All 69 teachers who completed questionnaires over a three-year period said they benefited from their involvement in the program, from new ideas and techniques, and from the help they received with problem solving. In this program, the induction team worked with first-year teachers to identify areas of concern and needed growth and to set goals. The teachers reported problems similar to those in a control group, but were better able to motivate students, to respond successfully to student misbehavior, to develop positive relationships with their students, and to view their first year of teaching in positive terms. Administrators said they had fewer student referrals, parent calls, and student complaints involving teachers in the induction program than with teachers who were not in the program (Varah, Theune, & Parker, 1986). A series of follow-up studies on the Wisconsin-Whitewater program showed that teachers in the program had a higher retention rate and more positive attitudes toward teaching than members of a control group (Manley, Siudzinski, & Varah, 1989).

Beginning teachers who took part in a teacher induction program in the Richardson, Texas, Independent School District reported that the program enhanced their professional competence and motivation (Brooks, 1986). Such positive BTAP outcomes appear to have lasting effects. Experienced teachers surveyed in follow-up studies by Odell (1990) and Rossetto and Grosenick (1987) continued to report positive influences of their participation in a BTAP. Induction team members report that BTAPs are beneficial to them and to the beginners they work with. Administrators in three induction programs (Hawk, 1987) reported that being a team member helped them grow professionally and better understand the qualities of good teaching, made them more aware of teachers' needs, and improved principal-teacher relations. Principals in a program studied by Odell (1990, p. 15) reported that "the presence of the program positively influenced the atmosphere in their schools by emphasizing teacher interaction and collaboration."

Effects of Mentoring on Beginning Teachers

After conducting research on induction programs in eight states, Huling-Austin and Murphy (1987) concluded that

> The assignment of a support teacher may well be the most powerful and cost-effective induction practice available to program developers. First-year teachers who were assigned support teachers consistently reported that they relied upon their support persons most heavily for assistance (pp. 35–36).

Other studies agree with the conclusions drawn by Huling-Austin and Murphy. Huffman and Leak (1986) found that 95 percent of teachers in one beginning teacher program considered mentoring an important element of teacher induction. Teachers in the Wisconsin-Whitewater Teacher Induction Program considered the mentor to be the key person in the success of that program (Smith-Davis & Cohen, 1989). Another group of researchers who studied state-mandated beginning teacher programs concluded that

> For many of our beginning teachers the most significant positive force on their experience was the peer or support teacher. The peer or support teacher was typically rated as highly influential early in the year and increasingly influential as the year progressed. . . . They were valued primarily as sources of practical information and secondarily as sources of psychological support (Hoffman, Edwards, O'Neal, Barnes, & Paulissen, 1986, p. 19).

In Minnesota, a majority of beginning teachers who were in a mentoring reported that they had examined and improved their teaching behaviors and had received social and emotional support, and that their mentors were effective role models who demonstrated qualities of excellent leadership (Warring, 1989). Additionally, 85 percent of the administrators in the schools where the mentoring took place said that the program was helpful to beginning teachers, and 78 percent of the administrators reported that the mentoring program benefited students.

Huling-Austin and Murphy (1987, p. 36) found that beginning teachers believed they "received the most help from support teachers in the areas of locating materials, student discipline, lesson planning, grading, establishing realistic expectations of student work and behaviors, and having someone to talk to/listen." Fagon and Walter (1982) reported that the majority of beginning teachers in their study gave their mentor credit for helping them gain self-confidence, encouraging their creativity, and familiarizing them with the school administration.

3 Developing an Assistance Program

There's no handbook. Nothing's written down. You don't have a clue what's going on. Just simple things. How to write a hall pass . . . absentee lists . . . the dress code for teachers. How are you supposed to know that without a handbook?

—A BEGINNING TEACHER

Before discussing the BTAP model, we need to place BTAP development in perspective. Because the content of a BTAP is actually professional development, it should be designed as part of the school system's staff development program. In addition, the BTAP needs to be consistent with the goals of the larger program and to be related to other staff development efforts whenever possible. Both the BTAP and other components of the total staff development program, in turn, should be consistent with the philosophy and goals of the school district.

As with the development of any program, the actual process of developing a BTAP will likely stray from the clear, sequential path represented by boxes and arrows on a flow chart. Sometimes the components of program development overlap or must be rearranged. Problems are a given, and problem solving is a natural part of the program development process. Yet many problems cannot be predicted and thus are not accounted for in program development models. Despite the problems inherent with program models, they can be useful as broad guidelines for program development. Program models suggest concepts and processes to be considered and adapted by practitioners. With that caveat in mind, we propose the process illustrated in Figure 3.1 as a working model for developing a BTAP.

Organize the BTAP Development Team

It makes sense for school districts with staff development planning councils to place BTAP development under the auspices of those councils. School districts without such councils must start by appointing a BTAP development team. The BTAP development team can include, along with staff development council members where appropriate, any educators who are knowledgeable and concerned about the problems of beginning teachers. The central office staff, building administrators, the local teachers' association, and teachers at-large should be represented on the team. Representatives from nearby teacher preparation institutions or state intermediate units who have expertise in assisting beginning teachers can also be asked to serve as consultants to the team.

Conduct a Preliminary Needs Assessment

The program development team needs to begin its work about a year before it implements a BTAP. In fact, we suggest the team begin work early in the school year prior to the year that the BTAP is to be put into place. Planning that far ahead of the practice provides the team with a curious predicament: They are charged with planning an assistance program for beginning teachers who have not been identified, staffed by mentors who have not yet been selected.

Despite the variables, such as the specific needs of the teachers who will be involved, that advance planning can be critical to the success of the BTAP.

Figure 3.1
BTAP Development Model

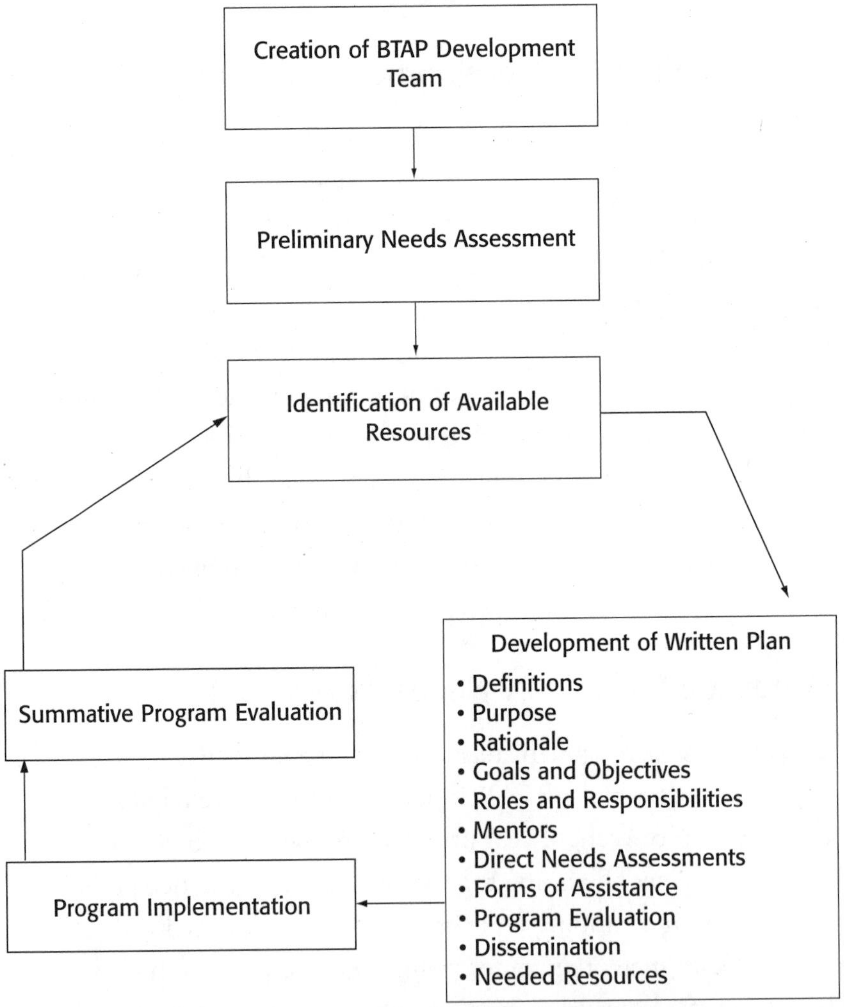

The team can begin planning by predicting some general needs of beginning teachers and mentors. They can gather information by reviewing literature on teacher induction and interviewing current first-year and second-year teachers to determine problems they experienced. Team members can meet with principals and supervisors and ask them to describe problems encountered by beginners they have worked with. The team can visit school districts with similar populations of teachers and students that have already implemented BTAPs to identify the needs the beginning teachers and mentors in those programs reported. And representatives from higher education and state agencies who have worked with beginning teachers in comparable school systems can also share the typical needs of beginners and mentors.

A preliminary needs assessment relying on these sources can serve as a basis for a broad, tentative plan for a BTAP. The plan can be revised and made more specific once mentors and entry-year teachers are available for direct needs assessments.

Identify Available Resources

Before the BTAP development team begins designing the program, they should think about available human and material resources. Potential human resources include educators within the school district who have expertise and responsibilities associated with beginners' typical needs, as well as representatives from teacher education institutions, state and community agencies, the local parent-teacher association, the chamber of commerce, and government service agencies. Potential material resources include available funding, curricular and staff development materials, and facilities and equipment that can be used for the BTAP.

Development of a Written Plan

The next step in BTAP development is to plan the program itself, and to put the plan in writing. According to Figure 3.1 (p. 24), the written plan consists of several components.

Definitions

The program development team needs to define key terms typically associated with BTAPs. These definitions should be consistent with the purpose, goals, roles, and responsibilities of the local program, not simply pulled from the literature or other school districts' BTAPs. A list of definitions might include terms such as *beginning teacher, induction team, mentor, mentoring,* and terms unique to the school system's BTAP. The team must make sure that references to those terms are consistent with the definitions throughout the written plan.

Purpose

The statement of purpose declares the BTAP's intent. It can be as brief as a single sentence, but it represents the vision on which the entire BTAP is based. Use the following sample statements of purpose to help write one that fits your BTAP.

- The purpose of the _____ School District's Beginning Teacher Assistance Program is to facilitate the growth of the beginning teacher toward the highest levels of professional and personal development possible during the initial years of teaching.
- The purpose of the _____ School District's Teacher Induction Program is to help the beginning teacher acquire the knowledge and develop the skills and attitudes necessary to experience a successful induction period.

• The purpose of the _____ School District's Beginning Teacher Support Program is to identify needs of the beginning teacher and to meet those needs through the collaborative effort of an induction team consisting of the beginning teacher, a mentor teacher, a university consultant, and the school principal.

• The purpose of the _____ School District's Teacher Induction Program is to facilitate the socialization of beginning teachers and to increase the retention of promising beginners.

Rationale

The program rationale is a statement that explains the need for the BTAP. Here are two examples of program rationales.

• The primary goal of _____ School District is to develop students to their fullest academic, social, and personal potential. One way to try to achieve this goal is to help teachers develop to their fullest potential as educators. A long line of research tells us that beginning teachers experience problems during the induction period, which, if not addressed, can lead to negative attitudes, poor instructional performance, and departure from the teaching profession. One group of studies tells us that beginning teacher assistance programs can solve or reduce the problems faced by new teachers, improve the quality of their instruction and their students' learning, and help us retain promising teachers. The beginning teacher assistance program described in this document is a research-based program designed to facilitate the optimal development of beginning teachers and the students they teach.

• Preservice teacher preparation programs are designed to provide teachers with the general knowledge, skills, and attitudes needed for effective teaching. Even the best preservice programs cannot totally prepare beginning teachers for many of the specific problems they must deal with during their transition to inservice teaching. Many new teachers, for instance, need assistance with adjusting to their new professional environment, organizing and managing their classrooms, understanding the curriculum, and obtaining instructional resources. The _____ School District's Teacher Induction Program calls for a team to work with the beginning teacher to identify problems and to help solve those problems. We believe that an induction team including a mentor teacher, the school principal, and a representative from higher education gives the new teacher the best chance to make a successful transition from preservice to inservice teaching.

Goals and Objectives

The results of the preliminary needs assessment allow the BTAP development team to state broad goals and general objectives for the initial year of the BTAP. A few examples are given below.

Goal 1. Mentors will develop the skills necessary to provide professional and personal assistance to beginning teachers.

Related Objectives. Mentors will develop

- needs-assessment skills
- communication skills
- problem-solving skills
- coaching skills
- conflict-management skills
- skills necessary to facilitate adult learning
- skills necessary to facilitate reflective practice

Goal 2. Beginning teachers will acquire the knowledge necessary to become oriented to the school and community.

Related Objectives. Beginning teachers will acquire knowledge of

- community history
- community demographics

- community resources
- students served by the school district
- school policies, procedures, and routines
- the school curriculum
- school curricular and instructional resources
- the school building where the beginner will be teaching
- the professional colleagues the beginner will be working with

Goal 3. The beginning teacher will develop or enhance effective teaching skills.

Related Objectives. The beginning teacher will develop or enhance skills necessary for

- managing the classroom
- planning, organizing, and managing work
- designing effective lessons
- motivating students
- diagnosing and meeting the needs of individual students
- using effective teaching methods
- evaluating student work

The goals and objectives in the initial written plan should be viewed as tentative. In fact, the program development team may decide to delay setting some objectives until the specific needs of the first group of beginners and their mentors are assessed. Once direct needs assessments are made, some revisions in program goals and objectives and corresponding revisions in the remainder of the BTAP will almost certainly be necessary.

Roles and Responsibilities

A comprehensive BTAP involves several support groups and individuals as well as beginning teachers. The responsibilities of each member of the induction team need to be agreed to ahead of time and continuously coordinated. The BTAP development team can use a chart like the one in Figure 3.2 to relate BTAP goals, roles, and responsibilities. Goals are written in the first column. The name of the group or individual who will coordinate assistance efforts for

Figure 3.2
Sample Chart Showing Relationship Among
BTAP Goals, Roles, and Responsibilities

BTAP Goal	Coordinator	Contributing Groups or Individuals	Specific Responsibilities
1.			
2.			
3.			
4.			
5.			
6.			
7.			

each goal is listed in the second column. Other groups and persons who will assist in efforts to meet each goal are written in the third column. The specific responsibilities of each party are listed in the fourth column. It's important to include the beginning teacher's responsibilities, relative to each goal, on the chart.

Mentors

The development team must decide on criteria and procedures for mentor selection and plan a program for preparing mentors for their new roles. Guidelines must be established for assigning mentors to beginning teachers and provisions must be made for ongoing support and rewards for mentors. These topics are presented in detail in Chapter 4.

Direct Needs Assessments

The tentative written plan for the BTAP is based on the preliminary needs assessment. Once entry-year teachers join the faculty, their needs can be directly assessed. And, once mentors begin to carry out their support roles, they will develop needs that must be assessed and addressed. More information about specific ways to assess beginning teachers' and mentors' needs is presented in Chapter 5.

Forms of Assistance for Beginning Teachers

The heart and soul of the BTAP is the support provided to beginning teachers. Many types of assistance cannot be planned ahead of time. But many can and—because of practical considerations—must be determined in advance. Chapters 6 and 7 present a variety of options for assisting beginning teachers.

Program Evaluation

There are two types of program evaluation: formative and summative. Formative evaluation takes place while the program is being implemented and it provides information for continuous program improvement. Major program revisions are not usually made as a result of formative evaluation. Summative evaluation is comprehensive and is done at a particular time, probably at the end of the first year of the program and again every three to five years. The summative evaluation determines the overall value of the program and whether or not major revisions in the program are necessary. Both the first summative evaluation and the formative evaluation should be designed during the BTAP planning process. If this is done, data for both types of evaluation can be gathered from the beginning of program implementation. Additional information on program evaluation is presented in Chapter 8.

Dissemination

The written BTAP plan needs to address four types of information dissemination. First, how will information about the need for a BTAP be provided to the community and educators within the school system? Second, how will the the plan itself be made available and explained to interested parties? Third, what provisions can be made to report on program activities that take place after the program begins? Fourth, what is the plan for disseminating program outcomes to the school system and community? By providing appropriate information to the school and larger community, the BTAP development team increases the likelihood of receiving support for the program and helps to ensure program success.

Needed Resources

A BTAP does not need to be an overly expensive staff development program, but it should not be an add-on program. Human and material resources already available must be developed and new resources must be identified and procured. The written plan needs to identify the resources necessary for each component of the program, along with a budget for each component. Hard money, rather than soft money, is necessary to make the program a long-term success.

Begin Program Implementation

Successful program implementation does not consist of merely carrying out the written plan in linear fashion. It involves a continuous cycle of implementation, evaluation, needs assessment, and program revision. This means that the BTAP development team needs to be available and active to sustain program development after the plan has been approved. Also, the initial program must have sufficient flexibility to allow for necessary change without disrupting the program or confusing participants.

Conduct a Summative Program Evaluation

The last component of the BTAP development model is the summative evaluation. A formal evaluation can indicate the need for minor revisions in the program or can lead into a new program development cycle resulting in major program revisions (see Figure 3.1, p. 24). Chapter 8 discusses the summative evaluation component in detail.

4 Mentors

Being a mentor keeps me current. When I have to answer my mentee's questions, it makes me ask, "Why am I doing what I'm doing?" In discussing philosophy, problems, or techniques with this new teacher, I find out what I really believe. That makes me a stronger person and a better teacher.

—A Beginning Teacher's Mentor

Mentoring is the cornerstone of many successful beginning teacher assistance programs. Although it is possible to develop a successful program without mentors, the mentoring track record is so positive that we advise every team developing a BTAP to include it as a component.

Recruiting Mentors

Where do you find mentors? You'll likely recruit mentors from the school's current staff. Therefore, to recruit mentors, you'll need to let the staff know about the need for and the purpose of the school district's BTAP and the role they could play in it. As you publicize the BTAP and the need for mentors, it is especially critical that staff understand that serving as a mentor is voluntary. Potential mentors should be made fully aware of the responsibilities they will assume if they become mentors. They should also be told about the rewards of mentoring and the support they will receive from the school system. Serving as a mentor can make a substantial difference in the careers of teachers (Ganser, 1997).

Several studies have documented the positive effects of mentoring on the mentors themselves. Warring (1989) reported that mentors in one program refined their own teaching styles and strategies as a result of being involved in the program. These mentors reported receiving social and emotional support from colleagues, as well as from administrators and other mentors. All mentors believed that mentor and mentee activities were productive.

Odell (1990) found that mentors perceived that their experience as support persons increased their confidence, broadened their perspectives concerning the school district, helped them gain knowledge about teaching and learning, and improved their communication skills. Godley and others (1986–1987) found that mentors believed mentoring enhanced the experience of being a professional and improved their collegial and process skills. These mentors felt that they had been recognized for their professional expertise and that they had made an important contribution to their BTAP committees. Additional benefits for mentors include enhanced self-esteem, renewed interest in their work, and new friendships (Gaston & Jackson, 1998).

In a preliminary analysis of an induction program for experienced teachers, mentors reported that they experienced professional growth through reflecting on their own teaching and through mentoring inexperienced teachers. These mentors also reported appreciation for the public recognition they received as mentors, their enhanced roles as teacher educators, and the increased colle-

giality with other educators (Killion, 1990). Ganser (1997) found
that mentors felt they had learned more in leading beginning
teachers than they had in participating in traditional inservice
education.

The best way to introduce your community to the BTAP and
the mentoring concept is at a school or district faculty assembly.
The next step is to offer a more detailed awareness session for those
who are interested. One possible introduction is to invite mentors
and beginning teachers from school districts with successful
mentoring programs to discuss their BTAPs in general and
mentoring in particular. Becoming a mentor should be represented
as a prestigious role awarded to those who possess outstanding
credentials.

Mentor Selection

There are a variety of ways to select mentors, including nominations
by principals or other teachers or by self-nominations. Those nomi-
nated by others should have the opportunity to accept or decline
the nomination early in the process. A committee should be set up
to screen nominations and applications. We prefer the process of
self-nomination and a selection committee made up of members of
the BTAP development team. In this system, mentor selections are
made in consultation with the school principal.

Prerequisite criteria and selection criteria are necessary when
choosing mentors. Prerequisite criteria indicate whether an individual is eligible for consideration by the selection committee.
Examples of prerequisite criteria are years of teaching experience,
years with the school system, level of education, and type of certification. Selection criteria are used to choose mentors from the pool
of eligible candidates. It seems logical to make those criteria consis-

tent with the literature on mentoring. Here is a brief look at what scholars say about the characteristics of effective mentors.

Schmidt and Wolfe (1980) conclude that the most important characteristic of a successful mentor is a commitment to provide personal time and attention to the beginner. They also found that mentors should have high professional achievement and have diversified interests and activities. Little, Galagaran, and O'Neal (1984) reported that effective mentors have personal and professional respect for those they are assisting; they are more interested in facilitating beginners than controlling them. Clawson (1980) found that those chosen as mentors were consistent, informal, willing to share information, and demanding. Positive traits of mentors revealed in a study by Gehrke and Kay (1984) were genuine interest in the advisee, helpfulness, caring, willingness to take time, dedication, professionalism, friendliness, outgoing nature, patience, and influence within the system. A study by Bova and Phillips (1984) suggests that effective mentors tend to evaluate situations from many points of view and examine multiple options for dealing with problems. Odell (1990) proposed that characteristics of effective mentors are teaching excellence; ability to work with adults; respect for others' viewpoints; willingness to engage in active, open learning; and social and public relations skills. DeBolt (1989, p. 19) used The Delphi Technique to have mentors themselves rate characteristics helpful to the mentoring process. The characteristics rated most helpful are

- approachability
- integrity
- ability to listen
- sincerity
- willingness to spend time
- enthusiasm

- teaching competence
- trustworthiness
- receptivity
- willingness to work hard
- positive outlook
- confidence
- commitment to the profession
- openness
- experience in teaching
- tactfulness
- cooperativeness
- flexibility

Ways of determining whether potential mentors possess positive characteristics include (1) reviews of letters of nomination or completed application forms; (2) interviews with prospective mentors and their supervisors; (3) examination of curriculum vitae or portfolios; and (4) reviews of written essays in which prospective mentors are asked to state their beliefs about beginning teachers, induction, and mentoring.

Choosing a mentor only when you are certain that a new teacher is going to be hired for a specific position is not recommended. Rather, select and prepare a pool of mentors, with the understanding that each mentor will be assigned a beginning teacher when an appropriate match can be made. If a mentoring assignment is not available immediately, the mentor-to-be might be given other support responsibilities, such as cooperating teacher, staff developer, or advising teacher.

Mentor Preparation

A lack of mentor preparation is the greatest problem we have observed in mentoring programs. A basic preparation program should be carried out before the new teachers arrive. Here are suggested topics for initial mentor preparation.

Knowledge About Teacher Induction

Mentors should be aware of typical problems experienced by beginning teachers and the purposes, content, and effects of BTAPs. The school system's BTAP and mentoring component should be discussed in detail. Characteristics of effective mentors and typical mentoring functions can be reviewed so that provisions can be made to identify and address any concerns participants have about the BTAP or their responsibilities as mentors.

Developing Trust and Rapport

Trust and rapport are the foundation of a fruitful relationship between mentor and beginning teacher. Mentors can learn how to establish a positive relationship by using open and supportive communication to respond to concerns beginning teachers may have about the mentor-mentee relationship.

Classroom Management and Effective Teaching

BTAP coordinators are often surprised when we suggest that mentor preparation include sessions on classroom management and effective teaching. After all, individuals chosen to be mentors are expected to be effective teachers and classroom managers. Yet mentors themselves are usually grateful that these topics are addressed during the preparation program.

Mentors know that they will be called on to model effective techniques for beginners. Many mentors have reached the stage of their craft at which they are unconsciously using effective management and teaching strategies. They often express the need to "brush up" on particular techniques. Analyzing these strategies during mentor preparation can help them to better articulate to beginning teachers why, how, and when they use particular techniques in the classroom.

The classroom management phase of mentor preparation should address ways to prevent classroom management problems and ways to respond to problems that may surface despite the use of preventive techniques. The effective teaching phase can include topics such as diagnosing student needs, designing lessons, motivating students to learn, addressing student learning styles, using alternative instructional strategies, and assessing student learning.

Adult Learning

The same methods a teacher uses successfully to teach children may not work when that teacher is trying to promote the growth of beginning teachers. The preparation program should address what motivates adults to learn and how to organize adult learning activities. Mentors can learn how to use the beginner's classroom experience as a resource for learning and how to make learning a matter of mutual inquiry by mentor and beginner. Finally, mentors can learn about adult learning styles and how to adapt mentoring to beginning teachers' preferred modes of learning.

Adult and Teacher Development

Research shows that cognitive, ego, and social development do not stop when a person reaches adulthood. Like children, adults pass through common stages of growth at different rates. Teachers progress through stages of professional development in addition to the cognitive, ego, and social developmental stages that all adults move through. An example of teacher professional development is stages of concern (Fuller, 1969). Teachers at the earliest stage of concern, the self-adequacy stage, are concerned about doing well when a supervisor is present, getting favorable evaluations, and being accepted and respected by other teachers. They are also concerned with whether their students like them and how their students evaluate them as teachers (Adams & Martray, 1981). The next stage of concern is the teaching-tasks stage. At this stage, teachers become more concerned with issues related to instruction and student discipline (Adams & Martray, 1981). Teachers at this stage are concerned primarily with their teaching environment and their teaching responsibilities. The highest stage of concern is the teaching-impact stage. At this stage, teachers are more concerned with student learning and students' general well-being. Academic concerns at this stage include diagnosing and meeting individual needs, sparking unmotivated students, and facilitating students' intellectual and emotional development (Adams & Martray, 1981).

Beginning teachers function at different adult and professional developmental levels, need different types of assistance, and respond positively to different styles of mentoring. Mentor preparation should include study of adult and teacher developmental variables, stages of growth relative to each variable, and characteristics of beginning teachers operating at each developmental stage. Mentors can learn how to diagnose the stage at which a beginner is functioning and adapt support behaviors appropriately.

Observation Skills

If problems develop that are going to cause the beginning teacher to leave the profession, the odds are that those problems are going to originate in the beginner's classroom. The classroom is "where the action is," and the mentor needs to regularly visit and collect information about what is happening there. Here we are not talking about checklists or rating scales used for summative evaluation, but rather the gathering of objective, nonjudgmental data that can identify the beginning teacher's needs and serve as a basis for instructional improvement.

One problem mentors and beginners frequently have is translating concerns the beginner may have about a lesson into observable, measurable behaviors. Preparing a mentor for classroom observation should include practice in linking general instructional concerns with specific teacher and student behaviors that can be observed. An extension of this training is practice in choosing or designing observation systems that allow the mentor to systematically collect data on select behaviors. We recommend that mentors develop skills for using a few simple observation systems. When there is no existing observation system that can be used to gather data relevant to beginning teacher concerns, mentors also need practice constructing tailor-made observation systems. Observation systems might collect data on the teacher's verbal behaviors, including types of questions posed, student time-on-task, classroom verbal interaction, and the teacher's physical movement around the classroom.

Interpersonal Skills

Glickman, Gordon, and Ross-Gordon's (1998) developmental supervision model lists three general interpersonal approaches used by instructional leaders. In a nondirective approach, the leader relies primarily on listening, clarifying, and reflecting behaviors. In a collaborative approach, the leader does more presenting, problem solving, and negotiating. The leader using a directive approach emphasizes directing and standardizing behaviors. Additionally, Glickman, Gordon, and Ross-Gordon distinguish directive-informational from directive-controlling behaviors. The leader using the directive-informational approach provides the teacher with considerable information and restricted choice. The leader displaying the directive-controlling approach determines the specific actions the teacher is to follow.

The Glickman, Gordon, and Ross-Gordon model holds that there is no one best interpersonal approach to use when supervising teachers. Rather, the developmental model calls for the instructional leader to develop a repertoire of interpersonal approaches and to match approaches to teachers' developmental characteristics. In this model, the leader uses a nondirective approach with teachers functioning at higher developmental levels, a collaborative approach with teachers performing at moderate levels of development, and a directive approach with teachers operating at lower developmental levels.

The long-range dimension of the developmental model calls for the instructional leader to foster the teacher's decision making. This is done by gradually shifting from a directive to a collaborative approach or from a collaborative to a nondirective approach during problem-solving sessions with the teacher.

Three interpersonal approaches seem applicable to mentoring beginning teachers: the nondirective, collaborative, and directive-informational approaches. (The directive-control approach does not seem appropriate for use by mentors in staff relationships with beginning teachers.) Preparation for mentors wishing to apply the developmental model can include the following phases:

- Skill development in each of the three interpersonal approaches (nondirective, collaborative, and directive informational);
- Instruction in matching particular approaches to beginners' developmental levels and educational situations; and
- Development of skills necessary to facilitate beginning teacher growth toward complex decision making and self-direction.

Problem-Solving Skills

One of the mentor's primary functions is to help beginning teachers solve problems they are bound to experience during the induction phase. Problem solving has been represented as a process involving several steps (Johnson & Johnson, 1982; Schmuck & Runkel, 1985). Here is a six-step version of the problem-solving model.

1. Gather information about the perceived problem.
2. Define the problem in specific terms.
3. Generate and consider alternative strategies for solving the problem.
4. Design an action plan to solve the problem.
5. Implement the action plan.
6. Assess the action plan and revise the plan if necessary.

Mentor training can involve participants in simulations in which they use the six steps to solve induction problems. The simulations and post-analysis of problem-solving exercises will, however, reveal that dealing with difficult problems is far more complex than the six steps in the process suggests. The process should be viewed as a starting point for examining problem solving, not as a cure-all for problems encountered by beginning teachers or mentors.

Specialized Training

A few examples of formal structures for assisting beginning teachers are coaching, action research, demonstration teaching, and coteaching. Assuming that some formal structures are selected by the BTAP development team for the assistance program, mentors need to be prepared for their involvement in those structures. For instance, if the BTAP calls for mentors to coach beginning teachers, the mentors need to become familiar with the phases of the coaching cycle and learn how to apply the interpersonal and observation skills of the coaching cycle. If the BTAP will involve mentors and beginning teachers in action research, mentors need to be taught about the action research process. Specialized training, then, is tailored to specific structures planned for the BTAP.

Planning and Time Management

Those who volunteer to be mentors accept a significant increase in professional responsibilities. A session on personal planning and time management can be a valuable addition to mentor preparation. Toward the end of the preparation program, mentors should be provided time to design and share tentative action plans for providing assistance to beginning teachers.

Matching Mentors with Beginning Teachers

In a study by Huffman and Leak (1986), 93 percent of beginning teachers indicated that mentors should teach the same grade or subject matter as the beginning teachers they are matched with. These same teachers, however, said they would prefer more competent mentors who did not teach the same grade or subject matter to less competent mentors who did. There are obvious advantages to having a mentor who works in the same school as the beginner, and additional advantages if the mentor and beginner work in the same area of the school building. Perhaps the two most desirable "matches" between mentor and beginner are those of personality and educational philosophy. The need for personal and philosophical compatibility suggests that mentors and beginning teachers should be provided opportunities for informal interaction before mentoring assignments are made, and that preferences of mentors and beginners should be considered.

Common Problems, Support, and Rewards for Mentors

Even when mentors are chosen carefully and are well trained for their roles, they often face specific problems that arise in nearly all beginning teacher assistance programs. If program planners are aware of these challenges to the mentor, they can build in solutions as they create the BTAP. Mentors need ongoing organizational, technical, and affective support.

One of the biggest problems facing teachers who choose to mentor beginners is finding time to provide high-quality support to a first-year teacher (Ackley & Gall, 1992). Even before beginning to help the new teacher, mentors must spend time training for their role. After that, time must be available for the mentor and beginning teacher to work together on a continuous, long-term basis(Bradley & Gordon, 1994). The two must have time to engage in collaborative planning, discussion, problem solving, and reflection. Both the mentor and the beginner need time to observe each other in the process of teaching. To merely add mentoring responsibilities to an already full work schedule is a disservice to the mentor and the beginning teacher, and almost surely lowers the quality of support provided to the beginner.

One solution to this problem occurs early in the process of setting up a BTAP. When choosing who will be trained to serve as a mentor, principals can select teachers who are not already overwhelmed with work during the school day (Young, Crain, & McCoullogh, 1993). The schedule can be arranged to include a common planning time for the beginning teacher and the mentor. In addition, teachers who agree to serve as mentors can be relieved of other duties to give them time for the mentoring process. Young, Crain, and McCoullogh (1993) suggest giving the mentors one free class period each day for mentoring duties. Finally, principals can provide substitutes or cover classes themselves to provide release time for the mentor and the beginning teacher (Smith, 1993).

Once mentors are given time to perform their task, they often find that their roles and responsibilities are not clearly defined. Some mentors experience conflict because their principals ask them to evaluate the beginning teacher. Even when a principal doesn't directly ask the mentor to evaluate the mentee, the line between mentoring and evaluating may become gray. Although mentors should not avoid collaboration with their principals, they should never accept the role of evaluator of the beginning teacher (Blank & Sindelar, 1992). The role of mentor must be understood by everyone. Mentors are support people—allies of the new teacher—and evaluation is not consistent with this purpose. The best way to avoid uncertainty of role and responsibility is to have clearly defined goals for your program. Establishing clear responsibilities and expectations on how a mentor will function in relation to the beginning teacher is an important step in avoiding conflict on this issue.

Many mentors do not feel supported in their role by other faculty members or by their supervisor. Sometimes there is a great deal of professional jealousy toward the mentor from colleagues who were not chosen as mentors. The BTAP program can provide ongoing support for the mentors through seminars or study groups. In this way, mentors and administrators meet to share problems, concerns, and successful strategies. They can discuss problems they encounter regarding mentoring or in their relationships with other staff members. In one study, Smith (1993) found that mentors viewed collegiality and mutual support from principals and other mentors as vital components of a program—not only for the success of new teachers, but also for the success of mentors. Seminars also provide opportunities for training beyond the preparation program and consulting with outside experts.

To best support the process of mentoring, the school needs to move toward a districtwide approach to staff development, in which all teachers and administrators support new staff (Watkins & Whalley, 1993). Fostering an atmosphere where all teachers, whether or not they are serving as mentors, are viewed as support personnel for the BTAP can go a long way toward eliminating professional jealousy.

Rewards for mentors might include extra compensation, stipends for innovative projects or professional travel, or release from nonacademic responsibilities. Perhaps the most important reward the school system can provide is public, formal recognition of the contributions made by mentors.

5 Needs Assessment

When you're a student teacher, if you have a major problem, you have the cooperating teacher right there to deal with it. You don't really have to confront the problem. Then when you're thrown out there to teach on your own and a problem comes up, you're stuck with it. You might have a student come right up to you and say something vulgar. What are you supposed to do? And later, how do you deal with their parents?

A BEGINNING TEACHER

The preliminary assessment (see Chapter 3) provides information for a broad, tentative plan for assisting beginning teachers. Once the BTAP is begun, the development team can assess specific needs of beginners and mentors, make revisions in the BTAP, and individualize assistance.

Informal Discussion

Regular opportunities for informal discussion between the mentor and beginning teacher facilitate ongoing assessment of the beginner's needs. Through active listening, the mentor can help clarify concerns or problems the beginner is experiencing. The mentor often needs to probe the beginner's perceptions to clarify her needs. For example, a beginning teacher's perception that students are unmotivated to complete seatwork because they are more interested in socializing than working may prove to be only partially correct. In this situation, the mentor could gather additional information by asking questions such as, "Are all students given the same seatwork or are assignments individualized?", "What specific types of seatwork are given?", "How often is the type of seatwork changed?", and "What do you do while the students are doing seatwork?" Based on answers to questions like these, the mentor and teacher may determine that students are indeed unmotivated to complete seatwork, but that the real problem is that assignments are at the wrong level of difficulty and lack variety, or the students need more individualized assistance. In this situation, the mentor can help the beginning teacher select appropriate assignments or develop skills to actively monitor and assist students engaged in seatwork.

Informal discussion can take place during group sessions with beginning teachers. Discussing beginners' problems and concerns at these sessions can help the program coordinator, development team, and principal assess school and district induction needs.

Informal discussion can also reveal mentor needs. The BTAP coordinator, development team, and school principal should meet regularly with mentors. Group meetings may often be brainstorming sessions in which mentors contribute ideas for improving both the BTAP and the support they are receiving from the school system.

Interviews

An interview is a formal way to collect needs-assessment data. It allows for more systematic collection and analysis of information about beginning teachers' and mentors' needs than informal discussion. Patton (1990, p. 280) distinguishes between the "general interview-guide approach" and the "standardized open-ended interview." The general interview-guide approach involves a set of topics chosen prior to the interview. The interviewer uses her own words to raise the topics during the interview, and asks those interviewed for their perceptions concerning the topics. The interviewer does not need to address topics in the order that they appear in the interview guide, as long as all topics are addressed during the interview. The general interview-guide approach allows the interviewer to ask probing and clarifying questions in addition to questions on predetermined topics. Spontaneity and flexibility are the advantages of the general interview-guide approach.

The standardized open-ended interview, in contrast, "consists of a set of questions carefully worded and arranged with the intention of taking each respondent through the same sequence and asking each respondent the same questions with essentially the same words" (Patton 1990, p. 280). An advantage of the standardized open-ended interview is that it tends to provide more systematic and comprehensive data than the general interview-guide approach.

Regardless of the approach, the interviewer records responses to questions either by taking written notes or taping the interview. Analysis of one-to-one interviews with beginning teachers or mentors can help to identify individual needs. Analysis of group interviews or comparison of data from a representative number of one-to-one interviews can identify needs common to a school or district.

Needs-assessment interviews of beginning teachers can be designed by the BTAP development team and conducted by team members or mentors. Mentor interviews can be done by the BTAP coordinator, BTAP development team members, principal, or an outside consultant.

Observations

Perhaps the best way for a principal or mentor to determine a beginning teacher's instructional needs is to observe the new teacher in action. The distinction between collecting and interpreting observation data is important to this step. Data collection should be based on the beginning teacher's concerns and carried out by the mentor in an objective, nonjudgmental manner. Determining a beginner's needs requires that the mentor and beginning teacher interpret the meaning of the observation data and identify differences between what the beginning teacher wants to happen during instruction and what is taking place.

Questionnaires

Written questionnaires can also be used as part of needs assessment. Questionnaires can include fixed-response and open-ended items. Data from fixed-response questionnaires are easier to analyze than open-ended responses, but they force the respondent to choose from a limited number of simple, sometimes artificial, responses. Open-ended responses are more difficult to analyze, but allow respondents to provide in-depth answers in their own words. Figure 5.1 is a sample needs-assessment questionnaire for beginning teachers. Refer to Figure 5.2 for a sample needs-assessment questionnaire for mentors. Part A of each questionnaire is a fixed-response section, Part B has open-ended items.

A Combination of Needs Assessment Techniques

Each of the four needs-assessment techniques (informal discussions, interviews, observations, questionnaires) has advantages and disadvantages. You may prefer to use a combination of the techniques.

Figure 5.1
Needs Assessment Questionnaire for Beginning Teachers

Part A. Please choose the response for each item that most closely indicates your level of need for assistance in the area described.

Possible responses:
- A. <u>Little or no need</u> for assistance in this area
- B. <u>Some need</u> for assistance in this area
- C. <u>Moderate need</u> for assistance in this area
- D. <u>High need</u> for assistance in this area
- E. <u>Very high need</u> for assistance in this area

1. ____ Finding out what is expected of me as a teacher
2. ____ Communicating with the principal
3. ____ Communicating with other teachers
4. ____ Communicating with parents
5. ____ Organizing and managing my classroom
6. ____ Maintaining student discipline
7. ____ Obtaining instructional resources and materials
8. ____ Planning for instruction
9. ____ Managing my time and work
10. ____ Diagnosing student needs
11. ____ Evaluating student progress
12. ____ Motivating students
13. ____ Assisting students with special needs
14. ____ Dealing with individual differences among students
15. ____ Understanding the curriculum
16. ____ Completing administrative paperwork
17 ____ Using a variety of teaching methods
18. ____ Facilitating group discussions
19. ____ Grouping for effective instruction
20. ____ Administering standardized achievement tests
21. ____ Understanding the school system's teacher evaluation process
22. ____ Understanding my legal rights and responsibilities as a teacher
23. ____ Dealing with stress
24. ____ Dealing with union-related issues
25. ____ Becoming aware of special services provided by the school district

(Continued)

(Continued)

Part B. Please respond to the following items.

26. List any professional needs you have that are not addressed by the preceding items.

_____

_____

_____

_____

_____

_____

_____

_____

_____

_____

27. What additional types of support should the school district provide you and other beginning teachers?

_____

_____

_____

_____

_____

_____

_____

_____

_____

_____

Figure 5.2
Needs Assessment Questionnaire for Mentors

Part A. Please choose the response for each item that most closely indicates your level of need for assistance in the area described.

Possible responses:
> A. Little or no need for assistance in this area
> B. Some need for assistance in this area
> C. Moderate need for assistance in this area
> D. High need for assistance in this area
> E. Very high need for assistance in this area

1. _____ Learning more about what is expected of me as a mentor
2. _____ Collecting classroom observation data
3. _____ Diagnosing needs of my mentee
4. _____ Interpersonal skills
5. _____ Assisting my mentee with classroom management
6. _____ Helping my mentee develop a variety of effective teaching strategies
7. _____ Using principles of adult learning to facilitate the professional growth of my mentee
8. _____ Socializing my mentee into the school culture
9. _____ Helping my mentee maintain student discipline
10. _____ Helping my mentee design a long-range professional development plan
11. _____ Finding resources and materials for my mentee
12. _____ Providing emotional support for my mentee
13. _____ Coteaching with my mentee
14. _____ Managing my time and work
15. _____ Problem-solving strategies
16. _____ Helping my mentee motivate students
17. _____ Helping my mentee diagnose student needs
19. _____ Helping my mentee deal with individual differences among students
20. _____ Helping my mentee evaluate student progress
21. _____ Engaging in expert coaching of my mentee

(Continued)

(Continued)

Part B. Please respond to the following items.

22. List any needs that you have as a mentor that are not addressed by the preceding items.

_____

_____

_____

_____

_____

_____

_____

_____

_____

_____

23. What additional types of support should the school district provide to you and other mentors?

_____

_____

_____

_____

_____

_____

_____

_____

_____

_____

Needs-assessment questionnaires can be given to beginning teachers and mentors at the end of the first month of the school year and again at midyear. Small-group interviews of beginning teachers and mentors can also be held after the first month and at midyear, allowing comparison of questionnaire and interview data. Mentors can observe classrooms of beginning teachers about every two weeks. Informal group discussions with beginning teachers and mentors can be held every few weeks. Informal discussions between individual mentors and beginning teachers can be daily, provided the mentor and teacher are based in the same school. Using a variety of needs assessment techniques at different intervals allows for comparison of data, which provides a more accurate picture of beginning teacher and mentor needs.

6 Forms of Initial Assistance

They just gave us our books and said, "Here you go."
—A BEGINNING TEACHER WHO WAS NOT GIVEN AN ORIENTATION

They went through the manual with us, instead of just throwing it at us and saying, "Here you are." It really helped.
—A BEGINNING TEACHER WHO WAS GIVEN AN ORIENTATION

The initial assistance provided beginners is an important part of the foundation upon which their careers will be set. Although not part of a BTAP, three items must be addressed before beginning teachers arrive if they are to have any real chance for success. Initial assistance to these teachers includes aspects of teaching assignment, workload, and work environment.

Appropriate placement within the district is vital for beginners. New teachers are often given large numbers of students and the hardest teaching assignments. Large, urban districts often place the newest teachers in the most challenging schools and classrooms. When they fail to reach students within this system, beginning teachers suffer from a sense of defeat and receive a huge blow to their self-confidence (Colbert & Wolff, 1992).

New teachers are often assigned classes outside their content areas (Huling-Austin, 1992). When this happens, novice teachers are expected to learn the content of the course as they learn to teach. Inappropriate teaching assignments can have far-reaching effects on novices and their students. For beginners asked to teach outside their areas of expertise, their growth and the education of their students can be disrupted. If new teachers do not have a good grasp of the subject matter, it is difficult for them to break learning into well-planned lessons (Huling-Austin, 1992).

Aside from teaching outside their areas of certification, beginning teachers often have multiple classes to prepare for, causing them a great deal of stress (Huling-Austin, 1992). Livingston and Borko (1989) propose that beginning teachers would develop teaching expertise more quickly if they were assigned fewer preparations, which means allowing them to teach the same content several times.

To help ensure success, new teachers must be assigned to students and content areas compatible with their preparation, experience, and abilities. Reasonable schedules, class sizes, and cocurricular responsibilities are all factors in an appropriate workload. In addition, the beginner deserves a work environment with adequate space, furniture, equipment, and materials. The most well-intentioned and carefully planned BTAP may not be able to overcome inappropriate teaching assignments, workloads, and work environments. If these areas are addressed, an effective BTAP can help ensure success for newcomers.

Celebrating the Beginner's Arrival

The hiring of a new teacher should be tied to celebration and demonstration that the professional community welcomes the beginner. Hirsh (1990) recommends inviting the new teacher to a contract-signing ceremony with district VIPs and taking a commemorative photograph. Other expressions of support include luncheons, dinners, and receptions with the superintendent, principals, and mentors in honor of new teachers. Holding ceremonies or social events expresses to the new teachers that a beginning teacher's entrance into the education community is significant and welcome.

Establishing Rapport and Building Trust

The principal, mentor, and other support persons must establish rapport and build trust with the beginning teacher at the earliest opportunity. Rapport can be established through open communication, clarifying and dignifying the beginner's concerns, and accepting the new teacher as a colleague. The new teacher's trust can be earned by displaying competence and professionalism as a support person, maintaining confidentiality, keeping commitments, and helping her experience success during the initial days of teaching.

Orientation

Beginning teachers can benefit from a general orientation for all teachers at the start of the new year. In addition, they should receive a special orientation that provides information pertinent only to them. A kick-off inservice day for all teachers may not deal with all topics that new teachers need covered.

The Community

New teachers from outside the community need to become aware of prevailing community norms, customs, and values. They need help acquiring an understanding of socioeconomic conditions in the community, and need to be made aware of community resources for teachers and students. In addition, they benefit from knowing about special community needs that the school is expected to help meet.

To help acquaint new teachers with the community, many school districts offer community tours. Others arrange a community orientation and social hosted by the PTA, school board, or chamber of commerce. A community resource file can be made available, including a map of the community and information on housing, public utilities, transportation, shopping, medical facilities, social organizations, and churches.

School District Policies and Procedures

Merely providing beginning teachers with handbooks is insufficient training. Teachers need to have policies and procedures explained to them, with rationales and examples. Beginning teachers need to be made aware of

- attendance policies
- salaries and benefits
- the teacher evaluation process
- their legal rights and responsibilities (as teachers)
- the role of the local educational association
- administrative record-keeping responsibilities.

The Curriculum

The orientation can include an introduction to the philosophy, purpose, aims, and goals of the school curriculum. An overview of the curriculum's scope and sequence should be provided with supervisors or experienced teachers leading small-group sessions on the specific content that beginners will be teaching. The new teachers should be shown how to use the curriculum guide and walked through at least one unit of instruction from the guide. Finally, beginners need to learn about available curricular resources and how to request new resources.

Information About the BTAP

The BTAP's goals, the role of mentors, and support activities should be discussed during orientation. A written program description can be included with orientation materials. Without a proper introduction to the BTAP, beginning teachers may misconstrue the program as just another set of hurdles to be overcome and the mentor just one more supervisor to be dealt with. Emphasizing the primary purpose of the BTAP—to provide support to beginning teachers—and giving specific examples of the types of assistance available can help to dispel misconceptions about the program.

The School

The principal and school-based support persons may wish to design their own orientation in addition to the district orientation. We recommend giving the new teachers a tour of the school building and a map of the school with key locations. Beyond learning about the building, beginners need to acquire a variety of information about their new school:

- Where to find out about available technology and applications
- How to locate, check out, and operate instructional media
- Where to find and how to fill out various administrative forms (and where to submit the forms to once they are complete)
- Where to find out about the school policies on student discipline and how to carry them out

- Where to find out about school guidelines on homework and how to comply with them
- What fire drill and emergency procedures are, and the teacher's role
- How to carry out student supervision responsibilities
- How to respond to student illness or injury during the instructional day
- How to record lunch count and attendance (and what to do with that information)
- When and how to secure parental permission for special activities or field trips
- What the makeup of the school's student population is, and how that affects the instructional day.

The Beginner's Specific Responsibilities

The department chair or team leader and mentor should be available to discuss the beginner's specific responsibilities. Beginners need to be given their class schedules, rosters, and information about students' past experiences and needs. Any cocurricular assignments can be explained during this phase of the orientation. Each beginner's classroom or classrooms can be visited, and classroom resources such as texts, workbooks, learning kits, and equipment can be previewed.

Informal Interaction

Not all of the beginner's orientation should be technical in nature. Get-acquainted and recreational activities can be planned as part of the orientation. Informal interaction with experienced teachers and other beginning teachers should be encouraged during meals, coffee breaks, or a post-session reception. Enjoyable group activities and informal discussions can go a long way toward making the beginner feel comfortable with new colleagues and reducing the natural apprehension that is part of being the new kid on the block.

Assistance for the First Week of Teaching

The first week of teaching is the most critical one for beginning teachers. The best way to help new teachers have a successful first week is to help them prepare for that week well in advance. Mentors can help new teachers create seating arrangements that promote effective classroom management and instruction. Classroom equipment and materials can be arranged for maximum use and efficiency. And, in preparation for that first week, rules and procedures for student behavior can be written.

Mentors can help new teachers by giving them advice on how to establish the classroom environment. For example, remind new teachers that they should present classroom rules and procedures on the first day of school, along with rationales for each rule or procedure and examples of compliance and noncompliance. Rewards for compliance and consequences for noncompliance should be explained (Brooks & Shouse, 1984; Gratch, 1994). Part of the flow of the first week is to give students opportunities to rehearse classroom procedures and receive feedback on their performance with reteaching provided when necessary (Evertson, Wide, Green, & Crawford, 1985). By creating a productive classroom climate during the first days of teaching, beginning teachers lay the foundation for a positive atmosphere for the entire school year. Beginners will be far more likely to establish this type of atmosphere with the assistance of mentors who have experience with appropriate rules and procedures.

Mentors can also help beginners prepare for teaching academic content during the first week by collaborating on the design of detailed lesson plans. New teachers can rehearse or describe critical elements of lessons to mentors. Mentors and beginners can discuss situations that might occur during lessons and alternative teacher responses. Each mentor and new teacher can meet daily during the first week of school to analyze the beginner's teaching experiences each day and revise plans for the following day. The first week is the most important time of the school year for the mentor to be available for the beginning teacher—the mentor needs to be ready to provide professional and emotional support.

7 Forms of Ongoing Assistance

Stress! You're teaching classes all day long. You're keeping students on task, you're testing, you're trying to follow all the rules—every principle and guideline that's set out for you. You're adhering to a schedule: you must teach all the things in the course of study by the end of the year. After school you go home and take your job with you. Then you must face kids who have homework and a husband who has had a tough day too.

—A BEGINNING TEACHER

Let them know that you've been there, that you've experienced this too, and that they can survive!

—A BEGINNING TEACHER MENTOR

The big thing is to be there, with an open ear, a shoulder to cry on, whatever they need.

—A BEGINNING TEACHER MENTOR

Beginning teachers need support throughout the induction period. BTAP development teams must choose from, adapt, and integrate a wide range of strategies to provide this support. The forms of assistance included in a particular BTAP depend on program goals, induction team expertise, available resources, and the beginner's specific needs.

Providing Moral Support

Moral support is one of the most vital forms of assistance the induction team can provide for the beginning teacher. Fortunately, moral support doesn't require sophisticated counseling skills. Just being available to listen to the new teacher's concerns and to help the beginner keep matters in perspective is of enormous benefit to most newcomers. Moral support can be provided during informal discussions between an induction team member and the beginner, during induction team meetings, and during seminars that include other beginning teachers.

Providing System Information

The beginning teacher needs to acquire an enormous amount of system information throughout the school year. After the initial orientation, the principal and mentor become the logical conveyers of most system information. They can extend and reinforce information initially provided during the orientation and introduce new information as the school year continues. Each month brings new information needs. The Pennsylvania State Education Association has designed a calendar of topics for a BTAP, listing information and suggesting which month each need should be addressed. A modified version of the calendar is provided in Figure 7.1.

One technique for delivering information to the beginner is an induction notebook. The notebook can be divided into sections, with sections containing information and materials for each month. A monthly newsletter for beginning teachers can provide timely information. Electronic mail can also be used to remind beginners and mentors of upcoming events and responsibilities.

Figure 7.1
Examples of BTAP Topics

MONTH	TOPIC
August:	Emergency Phone Numbers
	Schedule
	Getting Started
	Role and Responsibility of the Beginning Teacher as a Part of the Induction Program
	Expectations for Beginning Teachers
Sept-May:	Importance of Teacher Self-Image
September:	Role and Responsibilities of the Induction Team
	District Policies and Procedures
	District Philosophy
	Grading and Retention Policy
	Building Policies and Procedures
	Extra Duties
Sept-Nov:	Curriculum Guides and Planned Course Documents
	Informal Peer Interaction Guidelines
	Classroom Management
	Time Management
October:	Contractual Obligations
	Professional Obligations
	Inservice Education
	Professional Organizations
	Certification and Induction
	Discipline Policy
	Attendance Procedures
	Communication Between Home and School
	Parent-Teacher Conference Procedures
	Parent-Teacher Conferencing Techniques
	Characteristics of Professionalism
	Confidentiality
	Support of School System
	Support of Colleagues
	Ethics

Academic Freedom
Professional Demeanor
Record Keeping

November: Textbooks, Resource Materials, Community Resources
Library Services
Pupil Support Services
Guidance
Nurse
Home, School Visitor
School Psychologist

December: Field Trip Procedures
Extracurricular Activities

January: Federal Programs, including Chapter I and II
Organization for Instruction
Student Needs
Student Involvement and Motivation

February: Group Instruction

March: Slow Learners
Special Education Referrals
Gifted and Talented Students
Parental Contacts and Involvement

April: Goal Setting
Demographic and Social Structure of the Community

May: Materials Acquisition

This partial reproduction is from Steinhart (ed.) (1986). *Induction Manual.*
Pennsylvania State Education Association, Council on Instruction and
Professional Development, 6-9.

Socializing the Beginning Teacher

Beginners need to find out what is expected of them as professionals and faculty members, and how to meet those expectations. Serving as positive role models is one of the most powerful ways other professionals can help socialize the beginning teacher. Additionally, the mentor can make the beginner aware of do's and don'ts that have become part of the school culture over the years. The beginner also needs to be taught how to "buck the system" when necessary—how to advocate needed change without provoking negative responses from others.

Socialization is a two-way street. Professionals and nonprofessionals in the school need to do everything possible to break down the social isolation often experienced by new teachers. Early in the year, the principal can arrange roundtable discussions about school norms and routines involving beginners, mentors, and other experienced teachers. Beginners will be fully socialized only through extended interaction with other members of the school community.

Assisting with Planning, Organizing, and Work Management

Up-front planning and organizing for the school year can make the beginner's first teaching experiences as productive and enjoyable as possible. Mentors can help beginners design topical outlines for the school year for each content area. The beginner and mentor can collaborate in writing the first units of instruction and daily plans, and the mentor can review the new teacher's lesson plans throughout the first term.

The beginner will likely need assistance with classroom organization throughout the school year. The mentor can help the beginner rearrange classroom furniture and space, create new learning and resource centers, design systems for tracking student progress, and set up new classroom routines to accommodate changing curriculum and instruction.

One of beginning teachers' chief complaints is the tremendous workload they have, including a seemingly endless flow of paperwork. Induction team members can share tricks of the trade for reducing the time needed to create learning materials, plan lessons, grade student work, and complete administrative paperwork. Also, mentors can help new teachers track the time they spend on various out-of-class tasks and assist them in prioritizing schedules to allow more time for essential work and less time for nonessential activities.

Helping Beginners Find Resources and Materials

At the beginning of the school year, the induction team is responsible for ensuring that the beginner has all the resources and materials generally required for implementing the curriculum. After that, the mentor can help the new teacher procure necessary resources and materials for each unit of instruction. It may be necessary for the BTAP to provide special funding to ensure that beginners have adequate resources for effective teaching.

Holding Team Meetings

The induction team should meet regularly to review the new teacher's progress and discuss needs. Meetings allow team members to review prior support activities and coordinate future team efforts. These meetings can also be used to design a professional development plan for the beginning teacher. The plan should not be formulated until the beginner has had several weeks of teaching experience. The beginning teacher, with the assistance of other members of the induction team, should set long-range professional improvement goals and objectives. The team must agree on activities that each member will carry out to help meet the goals and set a standard of achievement. Figure 7.2 is a form for organizing a professional development plan. As the team continues to meet throughout the school year, progress toward the professional development goals can be discussed and, if necessary, revisions can be made in the action plans.

Providing Skills Training

Topics for training programs include classroom management skills, instructional skills, and skills for collaborating with parents. Joyce and Shower (1982) have developed a research-based model for skills training, which includes the following phases:

1. Presentation of the theory or rationale underlying the skill
2. Demonstration of the skill
3. Skill practice in protected conditions, accompanied by feedback
4. Coaching within the clinical setting.

School districts with insufficient numbers of beginners for skills-training workshops may wish to join a BTAP consortium, which can provide training for beginners from several school districts at the same workshops. An interesting variation of a beginner training program is a series of workshops attended by new teachers and mentors, with beginner and mentor in the role of trainee.

Coaching the Beginner

The beginning teacher can be coached by either the principal or mentor, although the mentor is more likely to coach the beginner on a regular basis. The following is a five-phase coaching model based on the clinical supervision model developed by Goldhammer (1969).

Figure 7.2
Beginning Teacher Professional Development Plan

Beginning Teacher_____

Mentor_____

Principal_____

Outside Consultant_____

Date_____

_____

Professional Improvement Goal_____

_____

Objectives_____

_____

Action Plan

Beginning Teacher's Responsibilities_____ .

_____

Mentor's Responsibilities_____

_____

Principal's Responsibilities_____

_____

Outside Consultant's Responsibilities_____

_____

Standard of Achievement_____

_____

Pre-Observation Conference

The coach and beginner start the pre-observation conference by discussing the learning objectives, planned activities, and student evaluation strategies for a lesson the beginner will be teaching. Next, the coach and beginner discuss concerns or interests the new teacher may have about the lesson. Then they agree on specific teacher and student behaviors the coach will gather data on during the lesson and select or design a data-collection system.

Classroom Observation

The coach observes the beginner's lesson using the observation system selected or designed in the pre-observation conference. Because the pre-observation conference agreement represents a contract between the coach and beginner, the coach collects only the agreed-upon data.

Analysis and Strategy

The coach analyzes the observation data and decides how to best report the information to the beginner. The coach also decides what interpersonal approach to use during the postobservation conference.

Postobservation Conference

The coach shares the data collected during the classroom observation and the coach and beginner interpret the data. The beginner may then choose an instructional improvement goal. At this point the postobservation conference can shift into a pre-observation conference as the beginner and mentor plan changes in the beginner's teaching, and structure a new observation to collect data on the improvement effort.

Post-Analysis

The post-analysis consists of the coach collecting and analyzing data about his own coaching performance for the purpose of improvement. Post-analysis includes oral feedback from the beginner, or the coach may tape the postobservation conference and review the tape.

Arranging Observations by Beginning Teachers

One of the most helpful benefits provided to a beginning teacher is the opportunity to observe effective teaching. The principal and mentor can arrange for the beginning teacher to visit effective teachers' classrooms. It is a good idea for the beginner to collect information on particular aspects of observed lessons. Some examples of things the new teacher might focus on are classroom organization, how the teacher opens the lesson, how directions are given, teacher questioning, student learning activities, and lesson closure. It is helpful to arrange visitations that allow the beginning teacher to observe different content areas, grade levels, and a variety of teaching styles.

Demonstration teaching allows the beginner to observe a master teacher using a particular instructional strategy. The master teacher can be the mentor or another teacher. The demonstration can take one of two forms—the new teacher can visit the master teacher's classroom or the master teacher can visit the beginner's room and teach a lesson to the students. The demonstration does not need to be limited to the delivery of instruction. The master teacher can also model what is done to prepare for and evaluate the observed lesson.

Coteaching

The beginning teacher and mentor are natural partners for coteaching. The advantage of coteaching for the new teacher is not just being able to observe a skilled teacher, but being actively involved with the experienced colleague throughout the entire process of diagnosing student needs, setting learning objectives, planning the lesson, and evaluating results. The beginner and mentor can coteach a single lesson or an entire unit of instruction.

Videotaping

Videotape is a powerful tool for improving the beginner's classroom management and instruction. A demonstration lesson can be taped so that the beginning teacher and mentor can review and analyze key elements of the lesson. Videotaping can also be used to collect classroom observation data on the beginner's instruction during a coaching cycle. The new teacher and principal or mentor can review videos of the beginner's teaching, freezing the tape to discuss instructional strengths and problems revealed by the video. One especially effective technique is to tape the beginner's instruction before and after implementation of an action plan for instructional improvement. The "before" and "after" videos can be used to observe the beginner's progress toward the improvement goal.

Fostering Reflection

One way to promote beginning teachers' personal and professional development is to provide opportunities for beginners to reflect on experiences, problems, successes, and future alternatives. There are several ways to promote reflection.

Journal Writing

Journal writing is an ongoing means of reflection. Critical events, emotions, concerns, and future plans can all be subjects for reflective writing, which can be done daily. The beginning teacher and mentor need to establish at the beginning of the school year whether the new teacher's journal entries will be private or shared with the mentor.

Nonevaluative Portfolios

A nonevaluative portfolio is a collection of items that form a record of the beginner's personal and professional growth. Student papers, photographs, especially effective lesson plans, and even videotapes may be included in the portfolio. Items in the portfolio reflect incidents, milestones, and successes experienced by the beginner. Reviewing the portfolio gives the new teacher an opportunity to reflect on events and become more aware of how concerns, attitudes, values, and behaviors develop and change throughout the school year.

Student Case Studies

All teachers have some students who are more difficult to teach than others. One way that the beginner can turn frustration into objective inquiry aimed at student growth is to carry out an intensive case study of an at-risk student. A case study involves gathering considerable information from a variety of sources on the student's behaviors and the reasons for those behaviors. The study should culminate in a reflective report, including a description of actions the teacher intends to carry out to foster the student's personal, social, and academic growth.

Review of Critical Incidents

Another way to encourage reflection is to have new teachers analyze critical events that occur at school. New teachers can describe events that have significantly affected them, consider the context of the event, and then think about why it had such a significant effect. After interpreting current feelings and concerns about the event and reflecting on what they have learned from the event, the new teacher is better prepared with ways to respond to similar situations in the future.

Study Groups

Study groups provide teachers the opportunity to meet and discuss books, journal articles, and new teaching methods. Aside from increasing beginning teachers' professional knowledge, study groups allow these teachers important opportunities to increase their communication, collaboration, and collegiality with peers.

As part of a BTAP, a study group can be arranged in many different ways. The study group could consist of all new teachers, facilitated by an experienced teacher or the school's counselor. The leadership role could rotate among the group members. In this arrangement, the beginning teachers' study group could read about and discuss areas of concern, such as classroom management, diversity, stress reduction, and time management. Such an arrangement fosters camaraderie among the new teachers and allows them to ask questions and make comments that they may not be comfortable posing or stating in front of more experienced colleagues.

Other study groups might be structured so that beginning teachers join a group of experienced teachers other than their mentors. Mixing the experienced and inexperienced teachers allows the new teachers to discuss readings and ideas and have interaction with more seasoned colleagues. A mixed study group allows new teachers to build a network of support outside their mentor relationships. Discussions with a group of experienced teachers can help the new teachers move beyond day-to-day concerns, such as classroom management and lesson planning, to higher-level concerns such as teaching methodology and fostering student learning.

Yet another study group arrangement is to have half new teachers and half mentors as participants. This arrangement would allow new teachers to discuss issues related to the early phases of the profession with a variety of experienced teachers to guide them through difficulties.

Whatever arrangement is chosen, study groups can increase reflection of the beginning teachers, while allowing them to increase their knowledge about teaching.

Collaborating on Action Research

Action research is a scientific approach to finding practical solutions to problems occurring in the school setting. It can be carried out by individuals or teams. Action research occurs within a BTAP when a mentor and new teacher collaborate to solve a problem in the beginner's classroom. The mentor and beginner engaged in action research should carry out the following steps:

1. Define a problem being experienced by the beginner;
2. Gather and analyze all relevant data using original sources (students, teacher and school records, and classroom observations) and secondary sources (theoretical journal articles, and research studies);
3. Form a hypothesis—a possible solution to the problem;
4. Test the hypothesis by designing and carrying out a simple and practical research study in the beginner's classroom; and

5. Analyze the data collected during the study to determine whether or not the hypothesis is correct. If the hypothesis is shown to be incorrect, a new hypothesis can be formed, and a new study designed.

This cycle can be repeated until a correct hypothesis is found.

Helping the Beginner Evaluate Students

One key to helping the beginning teacher evaluate student progress is to collaboratively create learning objectives that are relevant, at the correct level of difficulty, and written in measurable terms. Another important skill involves the use of varied, valid, and reliable methods for measuring student progress. Initially, induction team members and the new teacher can design measurable objectives and corresponding evaluation methods. The induction team can also help the beginner interpret information on student progress. After the first academic term, support persons can continue to review the new teacher's evaluation methods and grading procedures. Support persons can recommend methods of measuring student progress and guidelines for assigning grades but, as a professional, the beginning teacher must assume final responsibility for student evaluation.

Preparing the Beginner to Work in a Culturally Diverse School

Many new teachers find themselves working in schools that are far removed from their personal experience and background. A young teacher from a rural area might be placed in an urban school; beginners with no training in ESL may find themselves teaching students with limited English proficiency. Beginning teachers need help in working with liguistically and culturally diverse students. The induction team should be prepared to discuss the particular needs of the school's community with the beginning teacher early in the relationship. A professional development session on the topic of diversity as it relates to the individual school can meet the early needs of the beginning teacher (Barnes, 1993). The information given to the new teachers should be relevant to the school's situation and practical enough to offer assistance to beginners as they enter the culturally diverse classroom.

Teachers who have general knowledge of the school's population and cultural background can engage in formal and informal discussions with mentors and other experienced teachers. These later discussions allow the new teachers opportunities to ask questions and discuss problems as the need arises. Once the groundwork has been set, the new teachers can seek help in dealing with particular situations, students, and their families.

Preparing the Beginner for Interaction with Parents

The induction team can help the beginning teacher prepare for back-to-school night, parent-teacher conferences, and conferences requested by the beginning teacher or parents to discuss special problems. If a problem is serious or if the situation is emotionally charged, one strategy is for the mentor and beginning teacher to role-play a conference prior to the meeting with parents. Role-playing allows the new teacher an opportunity to practice dealing with issues that might come up during the conference, and allows the mentor to provide corrective feedback on the beginner's interpersonal style.

Preparing the Beginner for Summative Evaluation

We suggest that mentors should not participate in summative evaluation of beginning teachers. This does not mean that mentors should not help the beginner understand the district's summative evaluation system. The mentor can review the school system's evaluation instruments with the beginner, and even carry out "practice" observations to familiarize the beginner with what will take place in actual summative evaluation observations.

Conducting Seminars

The beginning teacher seminar can incorporate many forms of assistance. The seminar can be a structure for sharing information, discussing concerns, or planning for the future. It can be conducted by a mentor or mentor team, a principal, the BTAP coordinator, or a representative of higher education. Seminars can be held weekly, biweekly, or monthly. Despite the wide variety of topics that can be addressed at seminars, perhaps their greatest advantage is the opportunity they provide for beginning teachers to engage in professional dialogue, sharing their experiences and providing emotional support for one another.

Computer Networks

The popularity and availability of the Internet has opened new ways for beginning teachers to receive support. Electronic networking, such as chat rooms and online bulletin boards, can be used to support new teachers (Merseth, 1990). A bulletin board set up by a university's college of education or a regional service center can link beginning teachers with other beginning teachers, experienced teachers, and education professors. For example, a beginning teacher might post a question about a teaching method on the electronic bulletin board. Then experienced teachers and professors can offer advice and support regarding the situation. The World Wide Web and related electronic innovation has great potential as a tool for teacher induction.

Support Beyond the First Year

By design, the mentor-beginning teacher relationship is finite (O'Dell, 1990). It will usually end with the beginning teacher's first year of teaching. As the first year draws to a close, it is important that new teachers feel that they have a support network for their second year and beyond. The mentor must prepare the beginning teacher to disengage from the mentor-mentee relationship. Mentors can ease the transition by helping beginning teachers learn about the resources available to all teachers in the district, and they can encourage newcomers to find sources of personal support, both in the school setting and outside it (O'Dell, 1990). Mentors can introduce beginning teachers to a variety of school staff members, encouraging them to form supportive relationships with other colleagues. They can encourage beginning teachers to get involved in the professional development activities offered on their campus, such as study groups or peer coaching programs.

Inducting Veterans New to a School

The focus of this book is new teacher induction, but we do not suggest that experienced teachers new to a school do not require support. These teachers have some of the same needs as newcomers to the profession. Veterans, like beginners, need practical information such as when the bells ring, where to get supplies and materials, and how to arrange for a substitute at their new workplace. Experienced teachers new to a site, however, have other needs that are different from their first-year colleagues. Veterans need a realistic view of their new school. They also need to understand the challenges that inevitably surface when people experience the transition from one job to another (Hartzell, 1994).

Unlike beginners who are being inducted into the profession as well as to the site, veterans know what it is to be a teacher; they try to make their concept of teaching fit into the new situation. Their past experiences, positive or negative, affect the way they react in their new setting. Furthermore, teachers at the new school expect the veterans to be competent, while beginners are often given the opportunity to make mistakes. Experienced teachers new to a site are often offered little support, but they are expected to perform (Hartzell, 1994).

Several things can be done to ease the transition of veteran teachers to new a school. Veterans should be given a realistic preview of the new school and their jobs in it. Helping teachers bridge the gap between their expectations and the realities of the new setting can help them with the transition. The principal and the mentor should be aware of the nature of job transitions and build a similar awareness in the arriving teachers. It is natural to experience a period of adjustment in a new setting, and principals, mentors, and new veterans should be prepared for this eventuality (Hartzell, 1994).

Veteran teachers who are new to a school should be placed in situations where they have a chance to work with their peers. Placing them on interdisciplinary academic teams, in team teaching situations, or in other collaborative work groups can help experienced newcomers gain knowledge and respect from their new colleagues. Along the same line, principals and mentors should encourage these new veterans to take on responsibilities outside of their classrooms. Experienced teachers new to a site can bring new perspectives to committees and study groups already established on the campus (Hartzell, 1994). What better way for new veterans to get to know their colleagues and the way the school operates?

Finally, veteran teachers new to a school must be given feedback on their performance. If no formal feedback is provided, the veteran newcomers may not know if they are doing a good job. Principals and mentors should also arrange informal situations to discuss the new veteran's progress (Hartzell, 1994).

8 Summative Program Evaluation

The purpose of evaluation is to improve, not to prove.

—DANIEL STUFFLEBEAM

Be ready to listen to suggestions. Be open to change.

—AN EXPERIENCED MENTOR ADVISING NOVICE MENTORS

A comprehensive plan for assisting beginning teachers is the beginning rather than the end of successful BTAP development. Effective program development can be viewed as a continuous cycle involving planning, implementation, evaluation, and renewed planning for program improvement. The BTAP development model includes both formative and summative evaluation, which can be part of a continuous program development cycle.

Changes made in the program as a result of formative evaluation usually involve selected elements of the program, not major revisions. Eventually, a summative evaluation is necessary to assess the overall value of the program and to make any necessary major changes. Formative and summative evaluations, however, should not be viewed as entirely discrete. Much of the data collected for formative evaluation can be reanalyzed as part of a summative evaluation.

Purposes of Summative Program Evaluation

The purposes of summative program evaluation are to
- Judge the overall value of the BTAP and to determine whether or not it should continue.
- Determine minor or major revisions that should be made in the program.
- Provide information about the BTAP to interested stakeholders.
- Satisfy state requirements calling for evaluations of mandated BTAPs.

The purposes of the evaluation will in large part determine the scope and breadth of the evaluation.

Who Should Conduct the BTAP Evaluation?

The BTAP development team is the logical choice to coordinate the program evaluation. Team members may require technical assistance from the district office, state agencies, or university experts, but they probably can design most of the evaluation tools themselves. Beginning teachers, mentors, and principals participating in the BTAP can take on major roles in data collection and analysis. For instance, program participants can be asked to design questions for surveys or interviews, recommend documents or observations that could yield valuable data, and suggest alternative interpretations of collected data.

Evaluation Questions

The evaluation design depends largely on the questions that those authorizing the evaluation want answered. Here are some possible evaluation questions:

- What effect has the BTAP context (school environment, professional relationships within the school, school-community relations, and administrative support for staff development) had on the program?
- Have the needs of beginning teachers and mentors been correctly assessed?
- Is the BTAP design adequate for meeting identified needs?
- Have adequate human and material resources been provided for the BTAP?
- Have participants in the BTAP (including beginning teachers, mentors, and principals) been adequately prepared for their roles in the assistance program?
- Has each component of the BTAP been implemented as planned? If not, how has BTAP implementation varied from the formal plan?
- Have the intended outcomes of the BTAP been accomplished?
- What positive or negative unintended outcomes have resulted from the BTAP?

Data Sources and Data-Gathering Methods

A data source is a person, place, or thing from which data relevant to the evaluation can be gathered. Beginning teachers, their students, mentors, principals, other induction team members, other teachers, and school and classroom documents are all potential sources of BTAP evaluation data. Questionnaires, interviews, observations, case studies, pre- and post-measures, and document review are methods of gathering data from selected sources. Combinations of various sources and data-gathering methods usually yield richer information than any single source or method. Figure 8.1 is a sample evaluation questionnaire for beginning teacher. Figure 8.2 is a

Figure 8.1
Questionnaire for Evaluation of BTAP by Beginning Teachers

Part A. Please choose the response for each item that most closely indicates your level of agreement with the following statements.

Possible Responses:
- A. Strongly agree
- B. Agree
- C. Agree somewhat
- D. Disagree
- E. Strongly disagree

1. ____ I understood what was expected of me as a teacher
2. ____ I communicated often with my mentor
3. ____ My mentor was helpful in planning lessons
4. ____ I felt personally supported by my mentor
5. ____ My mentor observed lessons and provided feedback on my teaching
6. ____ I felt prepared to work with parents
7. ____ I became part of the school culture
8. ____ I received adequate assistance in securing needed resources
9. ____ I improved my classroom management
10. ____ I improved my teaching
11. ____ I felt supported by the program coordinator
12. ____ My mentor and I had ample time together
13. ____ I am glad that I was a part of this program

Part B. Please respond to the following items.

14. As a beginning teacher, what needs (if any) did you have that were not addressed by the beginning teacher assistance program?

_____

_____

_____

_____

_____

(Continued)

(Continued)

_____

_____

_____

_____

_____

_____

_____

15. What types of additional support should the school district provide to beginning teachers?

_____

_____

_____

_____

_____

_____

_____

_____

_____

_____

_____

Figure 8.2
Questionnaire for Evaluation of BTAP by Mentors

Part A. Please choose the response for each item that most closely indicates your level of agreement with the following statements.

Possible Responses:
  A. Strongly agree
  B. Agree
  C. Agree somewhat
  D. Disagree
  E. Strongly disagree

1. ____ I understood what was expected of me as a mentor
2. ____ I communicated often with my mentee
3. ____ I helped my mentee plan lessons
4. ____ I provided personal support to my mentee
5. ____ I observed lessons and provided feedback on my mentee's teaching
6. ____ I felt prepared to be a mentor
7. ____ I helped my mentee become part of the school culture
8. ____ My mentee's ability to work with parents improved
9. ____ My mentee's classroom management improved
10. ____ My mentee's teaching improved
11. ____ I felt supported by the program coordinator
12. ____ My mentee and I had ample time together
13. ____ I am glad that I was a part of this program

Part B. Please respond to the following items.

14. As a mentor, what needs (if any) did you have that were not addressed by the beginning teacher assistance program?

_____

_____

_____

_____

_____

(Continued)

(Continued)

_____

_____

_____

_____

_____

_____

_____

15. What types of additional support should the school district provide to mentors?

_____

_____

_____

_____

_____

_____

_____

_____

_____

_____

_____

_____

sample evaluation questionnaire for mentors. Part A of each questionnaire consists of fixed-response items and Part B of each questionnaire consists of open-ended items.

Measuring Outcomes

The open-ended questions in Figure 8.1 and Figure 8.2 focus on program outcomes. Intended outcomes are the program goals and objectives. Unintended outcomes are any additional positive or negative changes that result from the BTAP. Categories of intended or unintended outcomes that might be measured during a BTAP evaluation include

Personal Changes in	**Organizational Changes in**
• Knowledge	• Norms
• Skills	• Customs
• Attitudes	• Values
• Values	• Communication
• Concerns	• Leadership
• Daily performance	• Cooperation

The individual change categories can apply to beginning teachers, students, mentors, principals, and other program participants. Program evaluators may also wish to measure the BTAP's effects on the school as an organization. A program focused on a specific population may have schoolwide effects that are worth investigating.

What To Do with Evaluation Results

A variety of audiences are interested in BTAP evaluation reports, including state departments of education, the school board, BTAP participants, educational associations, and other school districts.

Different types of reports may be required for different audiences, with reports varying in length, the types of information provided, and language (technical or nontechnical). Evaluation results may indicate that the BTAP is largely successful and that only minor changes in the program are required. If the evaluation results indicate serious problems with the BTAP, the program development team needs to begin planning for major program revisions.

* * *

Education is facing a variety of complicated problems, many of which seem to have no clear solution. How to effectively assist beginning teachers is itself a complex problem. Fortunately, Beginning Teacher Assistance Programs provide a viable solution. Those of us who have seen the power of well-designed BTAPs have a twofold mission: (1) to make educators and other stakeholders aware of the serious need for assistance programs for beginning teachers, and (2) to convince educators and other stakeholders to commit the human and material resources necessary to make effective BTAPs a reality.

References

Ackley, B., & Gall, M. D. (1992, April). *Skills, strategies, and outcomes of successful mentor teachers*. Paper presented at the annual meeting of the American Educational Research Association, San Francisco. (ERIC Document Reproduction Service No. ED 345 046)

Adams, R. D., & Martray, C. (1981, April). *Teacher development: A study of factors related to teacher concerns for pre, beginning, and experienced teachers*. Paper presented at the Annual Meeting of the American Educational Research Association, Los Angeles.

Alleman, E., Cochran, J., Doverspike, J. & Newman, I. (1984). Enriching mentoring relationships. *The Personnel and Guidance Journal, 62*(6), 329–332.

Appelgate, J. H., Flora, V. R., Johnston, J. M., Lasley, T. J., Mager, G. M., Newman, K. K., & Ryan, K. (1977, April). *The first year teacher study*. Paper presented at the Annual Meeting of the American Educational Research Association, New York.

Armstrong, D. G. (1984). New Teachers: Why do they leave and how can principals retain them? *NASSP Bulletin, 68*(460), 110–115.

Barnes, C. P. (1993, February). *Beyond the induction year*. Paper presented at the annual meeting of Colleges for Teacher Education, San Diego. (ERIC Document Reproduction Service No. ED 356 225)

Bas-Isaac, E. (1989, November). *Mentoring: A life preserver for the beginning teacher*. Paper presented at the Annual Conference of The National Council of States on Inservice Education, San Antonio. (ERIC Document Reproduction Service No. ED 315 404)

Blank, M. A., & Sindelar, N. (1992). Mentoring as professional development: From theory to practice. *Clearinghouse, 66*(1), 44–48.

Boccia, J. A. (1989, March). *Beginning teachers speak out: A study of professional concerns in the first three years of teaching*. Paper presented at the Annual Meeting of the American Educational Research Association, San Francisco.

Boccia, J. A. (1991, April). *Beginning teachers speak out: A study of professional concerns in the first three years of teaching: Part II, Elementary teachers*. Paper presented at the Annual Meeting of the American Educational Research Association, Chicago.

Bova, B. M., & Phillips, R. R. (1984). Mentoring as a learning experience for adults. *Journal of Teacher Education, 35*(3), 16–20.

Bradley, L., & Gordon, S. P. (1994). Comparing the ideal to the real in state-mandated teacher induction programs. *Journal of Staff Development, 15*(3), 44–48.

Braga, J. L. (1972). Teacher role perception. *Journal of Teacher Education, 23*(1), 53–57.

Brooks, D. M. (1986). *Richardson new teacher induction program. Final data analysis and report.* (ERIC Document Reproduction Service No. ED 278 627)

Brooks, D. M., & Shouse, D. M. (1984, April). *Managing the first day of school: A component of professional training.* Paper presented at the Annual Meeting of the American Educational Research Association, New Orleans.

Cameron, I. M. R. (1994). Beginner's Tale. *Education in Rural Australia, 4*(2), 15–21.

Campbell,W. J. (1972). The teacher's view of teaching behavior. *International Review of Education, 18*(4), 540–546.

Clawson, J. G. (1980). Mentoring in managerial careers. In C. Brooklyn (Ed.), *Work, family, and the career.* New York: Praeger.

Colbert, J. A., & Wolff, D. E. (1992). Surviving in urban schools: A collaborative model for a beginning teacher support system. *Journal of Teacher Education, 43*(3), 193–199.

Corcoran, E. (1981). Transition shock: The beginning teacher's paradox. *Journal of Teacher Education, 32*(3), 19–23.

Corley, E. L. (1998, October). *First-year teachers: Strangers in strange lands.* Paper presented at the annual meeting of the Midwestern Educational Research Association, Chicago. (ERIC Document Reproduction Service No. ED 424 216)

Day, H. P. (1959). Attitude changes of beginning teachers after initial teaching experience. *Journal of Teacher Education, 10*(3), 326–328.

DeBolt, G. P. (1989). *Helpful elements in the mentoring of first year teachers.* A report to the State Education Department on the New York State Mentor Teacher-Internship Program for 1988-1989. (ERIC Document Reproduction Service No. ED 316 501)

Dussault, M., Deaudelin, C., Royer, N., & Loiselle, J. (1997, March). *Professional isolation and stress in teachers.* Paper presented at the annual meeting of the American Educational Research Association, Chicago. (ERIC Document Reproduction Service No. ED 407 384)

Earp, N. W., & Tanner, F. W. (1975). *A continuing study of the classroom and personal- professional attitude development of NTSU elementary graduates in their first year of teaching.* Research on Elementary Teacher Preparation, Monograph, No. 3. (ERIC Document Reproduction Service No. ED 126 002)

Evertson, C., Wide, R., Green, J., & Crawford, J. (1985). *Effective classroom management and instruction: An exploration of models: Final report.* (Contract No. NIE-G-83-0063). Washington, DC: National Institute of Education.

Fagan, M. M., & Walter, G. (1982). Mentoring among teachers. *Journal of Educational Research, 76*(2), 113–118.

Fuller, F. F. (1969). Concerns of teachers: A developmental conceptualization. *American Educational Research Journal, 6*(2), 207–226.

Gaede, O. F. (1978). Reality shock: A problem among first-year teachers. *The Clearing House, 51*(9), 405–409.

Ganser, T. (1997, March). *The contribution of service as a cooperating teacher and mentor teacher to the professional development of teachers*. Paper presented at the annual meeting of the American Educational Research Association, Chicago. (ERIC Document Reproduction Service No. ED 408 279)

Gaston, J. S., & Jackson, J. F. L. (1998). *Mentoring and its implications*. (ERIC Document Reproduction Service No. ED 426 990)

Gehrke, N. J. (1982). Teacher's role conflicts: A grounded theory-in-process. *Journal of Teacher Education, 33*(1), 41–46.

Gehrke, N. J., & Kay, R. (1984). The socialization of beginning teachers through mentor-protege relationships. *Journal of Teacher Education, 35*(3), 21–24.

Glickman, C. (1984-1985). The supervisor's challenge: Changing the teachers work environment. *Educational Leadership, 42*(4), 82–84.

Glickman, C. D., Gordon, S. P., & Ross-Gordon, J. M. (1998). *Supervision of instruction: A developmental approach* (4th Ed.). Boston: Allyn & Bacon.

Godley, L. B., Wilson, D. R., & Klug, B. J. (1986-1987). The teacher consultant role: Impact on the profession. *Action in Teacher Education, 8*(4), 65–73.

Goldhammer, R. (1969). *Clinical supervision: Special methods for the supervision of teachers*. New York: Holt, Rinehart, & Winston.

Grant, C. A., & Zeichner, K. M. (1981). Inservice support for first-year teachers: The state of the scene. *Journal of Research and Development in Education, 14*(2), 99–111.

Gratch, A. (1998, January). Growing teaching professionals: Lessons taught by first-year teachers. Paper presented at the annual conference of Qualitative Research in Education, Athens, GA. (ERIC Document Reproduction Service No. ED 417 170)

Harris, M. M., & Collay, M. P. (1990). Teacher induction in rural schools. *Journal of Staff Development, 11*(4), 44–48.

Hawk, P. (1987). Beginning teacher programs: Benefits for the experienced educator. *Action in Teacher Education, 8*(4) 59–63.

Hartzell, G. N. (1994, September). How to help experienced teachers adjust to a new school. In *Tips for principals*. Reston, VA: National Association of Secondary School Principals. (ERIC Document Reproduction Service No. ED 375 530)

Henry, M. A. (1988). *Project credit: Certification renewal experiences designed to improve teaching*. Terre Haute: Indiana State University, Department of Secondary Education. (ERIC Document Reproduction Service No. ED 291 681)

Hirsh, S. A. (1990). Designing induction programs with the beginning teacher in mind. *Journal of Staff Development, 11*(4), 24–26.

Hoffman, J. V., Edwards, S. A., O'Neal, S., Barnes, S., & Paulissen, M. (1986). A study of state-mandated beginning teacher programs. *Journal of Teacher Education, 37*(1), 16–21.

Houston, W. R., & Felder, B. D. (1982). Break horses, not teachers. *Phi Delta Kappa*, 63(7), 457–460.

Hoy, W. K. (1968). The influence of experience on the beginning teacher. *School Review*, 76(3), 312–323.

Hoy, W. K. (1969). Pupil control ideology and teacher socialization: A further examination of the influence of experience on the beginning teacher. *School Review*, 77(3–4), 257–265.

Huffman, G., & Leak, S. (1986). Beginning teacher's perceptions of mentors. *Journal of Teacher Education*, 37(1), 22–24.

Huling-Austin, L. (1986). What can and cannot reasonably be expected from teacher induction programs. *Journal of Teacher Education*, 37(1), 2–5.

Huling-Austin, L. (1988, April). *A synthesis of research on teacher induction programs and practices*. Paper presented at the Annual Meeting of the American Educational Research Association, New Orleans. (ERIC Document Reproduction Service No. ED 302 546)

Huling-Austin, L. (1992). Research on learning to teach: Implications for teacher induction and mentoring programs. *Journal of Teacher Education*, 43(3), 173–180.

Huling-Austin L., & Murphy, S. C. (1987, April). *Assessing the impact of teacher induction programs: Implications for program development*. Paper presented at the Annual Meeting of the American Educational Research Association. Washington, DC. (ERIC Document Reproduction Service No. ED 283 779)

Jesus, S. N. de, & Paixao, M. P. (1996, September). *The "reality shock" of the beginning teacher*. Paper presented at the International Conference of FEDORA, Coimbra, Portugal. (ERIC Document Reproduction Service No. 402 277)

Johnson, D. W., & Johnson F. P. (1982). *Joining together: Group theory and group skills* (2nd Ed.). Englewood Cliffs, NJ: Prentice Hall.

Johnston, J. M., & Ryan, K. (1980). *Research on the beginning teacher: Implications for teacher education*. (ERIC Document Reproduction Service No. ED 209 188)

Joyce, B., & Shower, B. (1982). The coaching of teaching. *Educational Leadership*, 40(1), 4–8, 10.

Killion, J. P. (1990). The benefits of an induction program for experienced teachers. *Journal of Staff Development*, 11(4), 32–36.

Klug, B. J., & Salzman, S. A. (1991). Formal induction vs. informal mentoring: Comparative effects and outcomes. *Teaching and Teacher Education*, 7(3), 241–251.

Kurtz, W. H. (1983). Identifying their needs: How the principal can help beginning teachers. *NASSP Bulletin*, 67(459), 42–45.

Liebert, D. K. (1989, November). *Mentoring first year teachers: The university's role as facilitator*. Paper presented at National Council of States on Inservice Education, San Antonio. (ERIC Document Reproduction Service No. ED 314 392)

Little, J. W., Galagaran, P., & O'Neal, R. (1984). *Professional development roles and relationships: Principals and skills of 'advising'*. San Francisco: National Institute of Education.

Livingston, C. & Borko, H. (1989). Expert-novice differences in teaching: A cognitive analysis and implications for teacher education. *Journal of Teacher Education, 40(4)*, 36–42.

McArthur, J. T., (1978). What does teaching do to teachers? *Educational Administration Quarterly, 14(3)*, 89–103.

Manley, M., Siudzinski, L., & Varah, L. J. (1989). Easing the transition for first-year teachers. *NASSP Bulletin, 73(515)*, 16–21.

Merseth, K. K. (1990). *Beginning teachers and computer networks: A new form of support*. East Lansing, MI: National Center for Research on Teacher Learning.

New Mexico State Department of Education (1988). *Preliminary report: New Mexico enrollment and teacher needs projections*. Santa Fe: New Mexico State Department of Education.

Newberry, J. (1978). The barrier between beginning and experienced teachers. *The Journal of Educational Administration, 16(1)*, 46–56.

Niebrand, C., Horn, E., & Holmes, R. (1992). Insecurity, confusion: Common complaints of the first-year teacher. *NASSP Bulletin, 76(546)*, 84–89.

O'Dell, S. J. (1990). *Mentor teacher programs: What the research says to the teacher*. Washington, DC: National Education Association. (ERIC Document Reproduction Service No. ED 323 185)

Odell, S. J. (1990). A collaborative approach to teacher induction that works. *The Journal of Staff Development, 11(4)*, 12–16.

Odell, S. J., Loughlin, C. E., & Ferraro, D. P. (1986–1987). Functional approach to identification of new teacher needs in an induction context. *Action in Teacher Education, 8(4)*, 51–57.

Osbourne, E. (1992). A profession that eats its young. *Agricultural Education Magazine, 64(12)*, 3–4.

Parker, L. S. (1988). A regional teacher induction program that works for rural schools. *Journal of Staff Development, 9(4)*, 16–20.

Patton, M. Q. (1990). Qualitative evaluation and research methods (2nd Ed.). Newberry Park, CA: Sage Publications.

Quinsenberry, N. L., Massee-Fox, S., Norris, W., & McIntyre, D. J. (1989). *Teacher induction: An annotated bibiography, 1985–1989*. Carbondale, IL: Southern Illinois University at Carbondale. (ERIC Document Reproduction Service No. ED 288 820)

Robbins, V., & Skillings, M. J. (1996, March). *University and public school collaboration: Developing more effective teachers through field-based teacher preparation and support programs.* Paper presented at the annual meeting of the Association for Supervision and Curriculum Development, New Orleans. (ERIC Document Reproduction Service No. ED 404 315)

Romatowski, J. A., Dorminey, J. J. & Van Voorhees, B. (1989). *Teacher induction programs: A report.* (ERIC Document Reproduction Service No. ED 316 525)

Rosseto, C., & Grosenick, J. K. (1987). Effects of collaborative teacher education; Follow-up of graduates of a teacher induction program. *Journal of Teacher Education,* 38(2), 50–52.

Runyan, K., White, V., Hazel, L., & Hedges, D. (1998, February). *A seamless system of professional development from preservice to tenured teaching.* Paper presented at the annual meeting of the American Association of Colleges for Teacher Education. (ERIC Document Reproduction Service No. ED 417 167)

Ryan, K. (1979). Toward understanding the problem: At the threshold of the profession. In K. R. Howey & R. H. Bents (Eds.), *Toward meeting the needs of the beginning teacher.* Lansing, MI: Midwest Teacher Corps Network, & St. Paul, Minnesota University.

Ryan, K. (1974). *Survival is not good enough: Overcoming the problems of beginning teachers.* Washington, DC: American Federation of Teachers.

Ryan, K., Newman, K.K., Mager, G., Applegate, J., Lasley, T., Flora, R., & Johnston, J. (1980). *Biting the apple: Accounts of first-year teachers.* New York: Longman.

Scheehy, G. (1976). *Passages: Predictable crisis of adult life.* New York: Dutton.

Schein, E. H. (1978). *Career dynamics: Matching individual and organizational needs.* Reading, MA: Addison-Wesley.

Schlechty, P. C., & Vance, V. (1983). Recruitment, selection and retention: The shape of the teaching force. *The Elementary School Journal,* 83(4), 469–487.

Schmidt, M., & Knowles, J. G. (1994, April). *Four women's stories of "failure" as beginning teachers.* Paper presented at the annual meeting of the American Educational Research Association, New Orleans. (ERIC Document Reproduction Service No. ED 375 080)

Schmidt, J. A., & Wolfe, J. S. (1980). The mentor partnership: Discovery of professionalism. *NASPA Journal,* 17(3), 45–51.

Schmuck, R. A., & Runkel, P. J. (1985). *The handbook of organizational development in schools* (3rd Ed.). Palo Alto, CA: Mayfield Publishing.

Smith, R. D. (1993). Mentoring new teachers: Strategies, structures, and successes. *Teacher Education Quarterly* 20 (4), 5–18.

Smith Davis, J., & Cohen, M. (1989). *Preventing attrition through teacher induction and mentoring and entry-year induction programs and practices: A bibliography.* (ERIC Document Reproduction Service No. ED 314 923)

Thomas, B., & Kiley, M. A. (1994, February). *Concerns of beginning, middle, and secondary school teachers*. Paper presented at the annual meeting of the Eastern Educational Research Association, Sarasota, FL. (ERIC Document Reproduction Service No. ED 373 033)

Varah, L. J., Theune, W. S., & Parker, L. (1986). Beginning teacher: Sink or swim. *Journal of Teacher Education, 37*(10), 30–34.

Veenman, S. (1984). Perceived problems of beginning teachers. *Review of Educational Research, 54*(2), 143–178.

Warring, D. F. (1989, February). *A collaborative mentor-mentee program based on the Bloomington, Minnesota, public schools*. Paper presented at the Meeting of the Association of Teacher Educators, St. Louis. (ERIC Document Reproduction Service No. ED 305 328).

Whalley, C., & Watkins, C. (1993). Mentoring beginning teachers: Issues for schools to anticipate and manage. *School Organization, 13*(2), 129–138.

Wisconsin Department of Public Instruction. (1984). *Final report of the state superintendent's task force on teaching and teacher education*. Madison, WI: Wisconsin Department of Public Instruction.

Wright, B. D., & Tuska, S. A. (1968). From dream to life in the psychology of becoming teacher. *The School Review, 76*(3), 253–293.

Young, T. A., Crain, C. L., & McCullough, D. (1993). Helping new teachers: The performance enhancement model. *The Clearinghouse, 66*(3), 174–176.

Resources for Practitioners

Chapter 1—The Problem: Unforeseen Difficulties

Huling-Austin, L. (1992). Research on learning to teach: Implications for teacher induction and mentoring programs. *Journal of Teacher Education, 43*(3), 173–180.

Marso, R. N., & Pigged, F. L. (1987). Differences between self-perceived job expectations and job realities of beginning teachers. *Journal of Teacher Education, 38*(6), 53–56.

Odell, S. J., Loughlin, C. E., & Ferraro, D. P. (1986-1987). Functional approach to identification of new teacher needs in an induction context. *Action in Teacher Education, 8*(4), 51–57.

Ryan, K. (1970). *Don't smile until Christmas.* Chicago: University of Chicago Press.

Ryan, K., Newman, K. K., Mager, G., Applegate, J., Lasley, T., Flora, R., & Johnston, J. (1980). *Biting the apple: Accounts of first-year teachers.* New York: Longman.

Veenman, S. (1984). Perceived problems of beginning teachers. *Review of Educational Research, 54*(2), 143–178.

Chapter 2—The Solution: A BTAP

Berman, P. (Ed.). (1990). Theme issue on teacher induction. *Journal of Staff Development, 11*(4).

Ganser, T., Bainer, D. L., Bendixen-Noe, M., Brock, B. L., Stinson, A. D., Geibelhaus, C., & Runyon, C. K. (1998, October). *Critical issues in mentoring and mentoring programs for beginning teachers.* Symposium presented at the annual meeting of the Mid-Western Educational Research Association, Chicago. (ERIC Document Reproduction Service No. 425 146)

Henry, M. A. (1988). *Project credit: Certification renewal experiences designed to improve teaching.* Terre Haute: Indiana State University, Department of Secondary Education. (ERIC Document Reproduction Service No. ED 291 681)

Lasley, T.V. (Ed.). (1986). Theme issue on teacher induction. *Journal of Teacher Education, 37*(1).

Liebert, D. K. (1989, November). *Mentoring first year teachers: The university's role as facilitator.* Paper presented at National Council of States on Inservice Education, San Antonio. (ERIC Document Reproduction Service No. ED 314 392)

Manley, M., Siudzinski, L., & Varah, L. J. (1989). Easing the transition for first-year teachers. *NASSP Bulletin, 73*(515), 16–21.

Quisenberry, N. L., Massee-Fox, S., Norris, W., & McIntyre, D. J. (1989). *Teacher induction: An annotated bibliography, 1985–1989.* Carbondale: Southern Illinois University at Carbondale. (ERIC Document Reproduction Service No. ED 288 820)

Robbins, V. & Skillings, M. J. (1996, March). *University and public school collaboration: Developing more effective teachers through field-based teacher preparation and support programs.* Paper presented at the annual meeting of the Association for Supervision and Curriculum Development, New Orleans. (ERIC Document Reproduction Service No. ED 404 315)

Runyan, K., White, V., Hazel, L., & Hedges, D. (1998, February). *A seamless system of professional development from preservice to tenured teaching.* Paper presented at the annual meeting of the American Association of Colleges for Teacher Education. (ERIC Document Reproduction Service No. ED 417 167)

Smith-Davis, J., & Cohen, M. (1989). *Preventing attrition through teacher induction and mentoring and entry-year induction programs and practices: A bibliography.* (ERIC Document Reproduction Service No. ED 314 923)

Chapter 3—Developing an Assistance Program

ERIC Clearinghouse on Teacher Induction. (1986). *Components of teacher induction programs. ERIC Digest No. 4.* Washington, DC. (ERIC Document Reproduction Service No. ED 269 407)

Hirsh, S. A. (1990). Designing induction programs with the beginning teacher in mind. *Journal of Staff Development, 11*(4), 24–26.

Huling-Austin, L., (1988, April). *A synthesis of research on teacher induction programs and practices.* Paper presented at the Annual Meeting of the American Educational Research Association, New Orleans. (ERIC Document Reproduction Service No. ED 302 546)

Huling-Austin, L., & Murphy, S. C. (1987, April). *Assessing the impact of teacher induction programs: Implications for program development.* Paper presented at the Annual Meeting of the American Educational Research Association. Washington, DC. (ERIC Document Reproduction Service No. ED 283 779)

Maryland State Department of Education. Research for Better Schools, Inc. (1987). *Perspectives on teacher induction: A review of the literature and promising program models.* Washington, DC. (ERIC Document Reproduction Service No. ED 288 587)

North Carolina State Department of Education. (1997). *Toolkit for mentoring.* Raleigh: North Carolina State Department of Education. (ERIC Document Reproduction Service No. ED 412 211)

Romatowski, J. A., Dorminey, J. J., & Van Voorhees, B. (1989). *Teacher induction programs: A Report.* (ERIC Document Reproduction Service No. ED 316 525)

Whalley, C., & Watkins, C. (1993). Mentoring beginning teachers: Issues for schools to anticipate and manage. *School Organization 13*(2), 129–138.

Chapter 4—Mentors

Acheson, Keith (Program Consultant). (1988). *Another set of eyes: Techniques for classroom observation* [Videotape]. Alexandria, VA: Association for Supervision and Curriculum Development.

Adams, R. D., & Martray, C. (1981, April). *Teacher development: A study of factors related to teacher concerns for pre, beginning, and experienced teachers.* Paper presented at the Annual Meeting of the American Educational Research Association, Los Angeles.

Appalachia Educational Laboratory, Tennessee Education Association. (1988). *Bridges to strength: Establishing a mentoring program for beginning teachers: An administrator's Guide.* Charleston, WV: Appalachia Educational Laboratory. (ERIC Document Reproduction Service No. ED 318 732)

Bas -Isaac, E. (1989, November). *Mentoring: A life preserver for the beginning teacher.* Paper presented at the Annual Conference of the National Council of States on Inservice Education, San Antonio. (ERIC Document Reproduction Service No. ED 315 404)

Bowers, G. R., & Eberhart, N. A. (1988). Mentors and the entry-year program. *Theory into practice, 27*(3), 226–230.

Costa, A., & Garmston, R. (Program Consultants). (1989). *Another set of eyes: Conferencing skills* [Videotape]. Alexandria, VA: Association for Supervision and Curriculum Development.

Ellis, J. R. & Radebaugh, B. F. (Eds.). (1987). *Theme issue on mentoring for teachers.* Thresholds in Education, 13(3).

Glickman, C. D., Gordon, S. P., & Ross-Gordon, J. M. (1998). *Supervision of instruction: A development approach* (4th ed.). Boston: Allyn & Bacon.

Hatwood-Futrell, M. (1988). Selecting and compensating mentor teachers: A win-win scenario. *Theory into Practice, 27*(3), 223–225.

Howey, K. (1988). Mentor-teachers as inquiring professionals. *Theory into Practice, 27*(3), 209–213.

Krupp, J. A. (1982). *The adult learner: A unique entity.* Manchester, CT: Adult Development and Learning.

Portner, H. (1998). *Mentoring new teachers.* Thousand Oaks, CA: Corwin Press.

Shulman, J. H., & Colbert, J. A. (Eds.). (1987). *The mentor teacher casebook.* Eugene, OR: ERIC Clearinghouse on Educational Management & San Francisco: Far West Laboratory for Educational Research and Development.

Thies-Sprinthall, L. (1986). A collaborative approach for mentor training: A working model. *Journal of Teacher Education, 37*(6), 13–20.

Warren Little, J., & Nelson, L. (Eds.). (1990). A leaders guide to mentor training. San Francisco: Far West Laboratory for Educational Research and Development.

Warring, D. F. (1989, February). *A collaborative mentor-mentee program based on the Bloomington, Minnesota, public schools.* Paper presented at the meeting of the Association of Teacher Educators, St. Louis. (ERIC Document Reproduction Service No. ED 305 328)

Zimpher, N. L. & Rieger, S. R. (1988). Mentor teachers: What are the issues? *Theory into Practice, 27*(3), 175–182.

Chapter 5—Needs Assessment

Cunnigham. S., & Nieminen, G. (1986, November). *Teacher today: Identifying staff development needs.* Paper presented at the Annual Conference of the National Council of States on Inservice Education, Nashville. (ERIC Document Reproduction Service No. ED 275 659)

Levy, J. (1987, July). *A study of the beginning teachers in Virginia.* Paper presented at the World Assembly of the International Council on Education for Teaching. Eindhoven, Netherlands. (ERIC Document Reproduction Service No. ED 287 799)

Odell, S. J., Loughlin, C. E., & Ferraro, D. P. (1986-1987). Functional approach to identification of new teacher needs in an induction context. *Action in Teacher Education, 8*(4), 51–57.

Quisenberry, N. L., Massee-Fox, S., Norris, W., & McIntyre, D. J. (1989). *Teacher induction: An annotated bibliography, 1985-1989.* Carbondale: Southern Illinois University at Carbondale. (ERIC Document Reproduction Service No. ED 288 820)

Chapter 6—Forms of Initial Assistance

Brock, B. L., & Grady, M. L. (1997). *From first-year to first-rate: Principals guiding beginning teachers.* Thousand Oaks, CA: Corwin Press.

Brooks, D. M. (1985). The teacher's communicative competence: The first day of school. *Theory into Practice, 24*(1), 63–70.

Emmer, E., Evertson, C., & Anderson, L. (1980, May). Effective classroom management at the beginning of the school year. *The Elementary School Journal, 80*(5), 219–231.

Kurtz, W. H. (1983). How the principal can help beginning teachers. *NASSP Bulletin, 67*(459), 42–45.

Littleton, P., & Littleton, M. (1988). Induction programs for beginning teachers. *The Clearing House, 62*(1), 36–38.

Chapter 7—Forms of Ongoing Assistance

Acheson, Keith (Program Consultant). (1988). *Another set of eyes: Techniques for classroom observation* [Videotape]. Alexandria, VA: Association for Supervision and Curriculum Development.

Barnes, C. P. (1993, February). *Beyond the induction year.* Paper presented at the annual meeting of Colleges for Teacher Education, San Diego. (ERIC Document Reproduction Service No. ED 356 225)

Bas -Isaac, E. (1989, November). *Mentoring: A life preserver for the beginning teacher.* Paper presented at the Annual Conference of the National Council of States on Inservice Education, San Antonio. (ERIC Document Reproduction Service No. ED 315 404)

Berman, P. (Ed.). (1987). Theme issue on peer coaching. *Journal of Staff Development, 8*(1).

Brandt, R. (Ed.). (1987). Theme issue on the coaching of teaching. *Educational Leadership, 44*(5).

Brandt, R. (Ed.). (1982). Theme issue on the coaching of teaching. *Educational Leadership, 40*(1).

Carter, K. (1988). Using cases to frame mentor-novice conversations about teaching. *Theory into Practice, 27*(3), 226–230.

Emrick, W. S. (1989, March). *Mentoring and peer coaching: An action model.* Paper presented at the Annual Meeting of the American Association of School Administrators, Orlando. (ERIC Document Reproduction Service No. ED 307 627)

Hartzell, G. N. (1994, September). *How to help experienced teachers adjust to a new school: Tips for principals.* Reston, VA: National Association of Secondary School Principals. (ERIC Document Reproduction Service No. ED 375 530)

Hunter, J. H. (1988, November). *Induction of new teachers: An Annotated Bibliography.* South Bend, Indiana University. (ERIC Document Reproduction Service No. 304 428)

Joyce, B., & Showers, B. (1982). The coaching of teaching. *Educational Leadership, 40*(1), 4–8, 10.

Manley, M., Siudzinski, L., & Varah, L. J. (1989). Easing the transition for first-year teachers. *NASSP Bulletin, 73*(515), 16–21.

Merseth, K. K. (1990). *Beginning teachers and computer networks: A new form of support.* East Lansing, MI: National Center for Research on Teacher Learning.

Miller, D. M., & Pine, G. V. (1990). Advancing professional inquiry for educational improvement through action research. *Journal of Staff Development, 11*(3), 56–61.

Oliver, B. (1980). Action Research for Inservice Training. *Educational Leadership, 37*(5), 394–395.

Wolfe, Pat (Program Consultant). (1988). *Catch them being good: Reinforcement in the classroom* [Videotape]. Alexandria, VA: Association for Supervision and Curriculum Development.

Wolfe, Pat (Program Consultant). (1988). *Classroom management* [Videotape]. Alexandria, VA: Association for Supervision and Curriculum Development.

Wolfe, Pat, & Robbins, Pam (Program Consultants). (1989). *Opening doors: An introduction to peer coaching* [Videotape]. Alexandria, VA: Association for Supervision and Curriculum Development.

Yinger, R. J. (1980, January). A study of teacher planning. *Elementary School Journal, 80*(3), 107–127.

Chapter 8—Summative Program Evaluation

Berman, P. (Ed.). (1982). Theme issue on evaluation of staff development programs. *Journal of Staff Development, 3*(1).

Epstein, A. S. (1988). A no frills approach to program evaluation. *High Scope Resources, 7*(1), 1–12.

Hamilton, S. F. (1980). Evaluating your own program. *Educational Leadership, 37*(6), 545–551.

Loucks-Horsley, S., Harding, C. K., Arbuckle, M. A., Murray, L. B., Dubea, C., & Williams, M.K. (1987). *Evaluating professional development programs. In Continuing to learn.* Andover, MA: The Regional Laboratory for Educational Improvement of the Northeast and Islands.

Quisenberry, N. L., Massee-Fox, S., Norris, W., & McIntyre, D. J. (1989). *Teacher induction: An annotated bibliography, 1985-1989.* Carbondale: Southern Illinois University at Carbondale. (ERIC Document Reproduction Service No. ED 288 820)

Stufflebeam, D. (1981). *Standards for evaluations of educational programs, projects, and materials.* New York: McGraw-Hill.

Index

About the Authors

Stephen P. Gordon is associate professor at University of South Florida. He is coauthor of a popular text on instructional supervision and has coauthored several chapters and articles on instructional leadership and professional development. Gordon has chaired a state task force on teacher induction and has assisted many school districts in the development of beginning teacher assistance programs and professional development programs. Gordon can be contacted at Department of Leadership Development, University of South Florida, 4202 Fowler Ave., Tampa, FL 33620-5650. Phone (813) 974-3420.

Susan Maxey received her master's at Southwest Texas Sate University in San Marcos, Texas. She teaches Humanities, a combined language arts and social studies block, at the Austin Jewish Community Day School in Austin, Texas. Maxey is a copy editor for the magazines *Scientific American Discovering Archaeology and Egypt Revealed*. She is also a freelance writer. Maxey may be contacted by e-mail at smaxey@austin.rr.com.

Related ASCD Resources: Beginning Teachers

ASCD stock numbers are noted in parentheses.

Audiotapes

New Teacher Induction Program: Practical Strategies for New Teachers by Michael La Raus (#200172)
Mentoring: Celebrating and Nurturing the Novice Teacher (#200198)
Mentoring the New Staff Member: The Foundation for Long-Term Professional Learning (#200085)

Print Products

A Better Beginning: Supporting and Mentoring New Teachers by Marge Scherer (# 199236)

Videotapes

Mentoring the New Teacher by James B. Rowley and Patricia M. Hart [series of 9 tapes] (#494002)

For additional resources, visit us on the World Wide Web (http://www.ascd.org), send an e-mail message to member@ascd.org, call the ASCD Service Center (1-800-933-ASCD or 703-578-9600, then press 2), send a fax to 703-575-5400, or write to Information Services, ASCD, 1703 N. Beauregard St., Alexandria, VA 22311-1714 USA.